BFI FILM

....

RoL

SERIES EDITOR

Edward Buscombe, Colin MacCabe and David Meeker

SERIES CONSULTANTS

Cinema is a fragile medium. Many of the great films now exist, if at all, in damaged or incomplete prints. Concerned about the deterioration in the physical state of our film heritage, the National Film and Television Archive, part of the British Film Institute's Collections Department, has compiled a list of 360 key works in the history of the cinema. The long-term goal of the Archive is to build a collection of perfect showprints of these films, which will then be screened regularly at the National Film Theatre in London in a year-round repertory.

BFI Film Classics is a series of books intended to introduce, interpret and honour these 360 films. Critics, scholars, novelists and those distinguished in the arts have been invited to write on a film of their choice, drawn from the Archive's list. The numerous illustrations have been made specially from the Archive's own prints.

With new titles published each year, the BFI Film Classics series is a unique, authoritative and highly readable guide to the masterpieces of world cinema.

The best movie publishing idea of the [past] decade.
Philip French, *The Observer*

A remarkable series which does all kinds of varied and divergent things.
Michael Wood, *Sight and Sound*

Exquisitely dimensioned...magnificently concentrated examples of freeform critical poetry.
Uncut

BFI FILM CLASSICS

METROPOLIS

. . . .

Thomas Elsaesser

A BFI book published by Palgrave Macmillan

First published in 2000 by the
BRITISH FILM INSTITUTE
21 Stephen Street, London W1P 2LN

Reprinted 2003, 2005, 2008

The British Film Institute
promotes greater understanding
and appreciation of, and
access to, film and moving image
culture in the UK.

British Library Cataloguing-in-Publication Data
A catalogue record for this book is available from the British Library

ISBN 0–85170–777–7/978–0–85170–777–8

Series design by
Andrew Barron & Collis Clements Associates

Typeset in Fournier and Franklin Gothic by
D R Bungay Associates, Burghfield, Berks

Printed in China

CONTENTS

. . . .

ACKNOWLEDGMENTS
. . . .

Anyone writing about a 'classic' is indebted to the generations that have made it so. My debt to the film historians and critics of Lang, von Harbou and *Metropolis* is recorded in the Bibliography. But there are also other kinds of gratitude to record: to Richard Combs who asked me to review the Moroder version for the *Monthly Film Bulletin*, to Irmbert Schenk who invited me to a symposium on the 'jungle of the cities', and to Malte Hagener for doing on that occasion an excellent job of translating my text into printable German. I want to record here the work of Ann Drummond and Leon Hunt on *Metropolis*, and above all, Heide Schönemann's uniquely valuable and still under-appreciated comparative study of the sources of Lang's 1920s iconography.

With pleasure I recall one memorable conversation with Tony Kaes on the ramparts of Lucca, the patient assistance by Tarja Laine, especially with the pictures, and Alison McMahan's very useful translation of Leonardo Quaresima's article from the Spanish, after Leonardo had been kind enough to send it to me. Sally Shafto sent me material from Paris, Rainer Rother from Berlin, and Kay Hoffmann was as indefatigable as he was ingenious in ferreting out the most recondite items he could find to prove that *Metropolis* was indeed alive and well.

To put me right on the different versions, I benefited from long discussions with Martin Koerber, who also showed me his chapters, while Enno Patalas graciously lent me the annotated chronology of his restoration. Hans Helmut Prinzler made sure that the Library of the Stiftung Deutsche Kinemathek was open to me, where the staff and Walter Theis accommodated my requests. Michael Wedel read the manuscript, and Rob White, hawk-eyed and utterly experienced, steered the book through the inevitable currents, always with a firm hand on the tiller (and the word-count).

Amsterdam, March/April 2000

INTRODUCTION:
'METROPOLIS' FOREVER, MORE THAN EVER
. . . .

Urban Modernity, Berlin's 'Golden Twenties', the Cinematic City: no film evokes these clichés of the past century more vividly than *Metropolis*, Fritz Lang's flawed masterpiece from 1926–7. Feeding on its own contradictions, this film classic has, from its own time to the present, trailed as many clouds of glory as frowns of disapproval. Lang's fatal UFA suicide mission in the studio's fierce battle with Hollywood became a monster-film the critics loved to hate. Some sixty years later, it took on the status of an *Ur-text* of cinematic postmodernity, the epitome of a sensibility its authors probably would have disapproved of: retrofitted techno-kitsch, and thus the archetype of a movie genre they could not have imagined, the sci-fi *noir* disaster movie. Generally recognised as the fetish-image of all city and cyborg futures, the once dystopian *Metropolis* now speaks of vitality and the body electric, fusing human and machine energy, its sleek figures animated more by high-voltage fluorescence than Expressionism's dark demonic urges.

Among the many creative hands and minds that have had the wit to put some heart back into *Metropolis*, a fair share of credit must go to Giorgio Moroder, the Italian composer of Hollywood hit songs and famous soundtracks from the late 70s and early 80s. In his mimetic admiration for the film he was, however, preceded by two English

Vaulting Ambition or A Tower of Crowns: *Metropolis*'s landmark building credits

directors: Ridley Scott, who in *Blade Runner* (1982) gave both story and setting of *Metropolis* an unforgettably vivid makeover, and Alan Parker, who was the first to spot the music video that had been slumbering undetected in Lang's opening scene all along, pastiching it to good effect in the 'We don't need no education' number of *Pink Floyd The Wall* (also 1982).

Dipped in the neon-Gothic light of *fin du vingtième siècle* decadence, there is indeed much for contemporary anxieties to thrill to: the troglodyte workers remind us not only of docile-looking but inwardly rebellious adolescents in school-uniforms, they also recall the drill-routines of boot-camp basic training. The metallic figure of the robot Maria now takes on features of 'girl power' where its original audience might only have sensed misogynist projections of malevolence. The boldly outlandish sets of *Metropolis*'s cityscape pulsate with consumerist life, compared to the stark modernist high-rises gone soulless and drab that once were its real-life contemporaries. In the contrast between the master of the city's high-tech office – the penthouse dream of every yuppie trader with a view to kill for – and the alchemist's lab that is home to the wizard Rotwang, multinational corporate culture meets new-age ecology and internet hacker culture. Meanwhile, down in the catacombs of *Metropolis*, with their secret mass-sermons of the saviour to come, the sweatshops of Asia and Latin America are only a shout and a prayer away from the religious fundamentalisms, the media evangelisms and voodoo revivalisms that have been fevering towards the Millennium.

Freder among the signs of consumerist life

Maria praying for the
Millennial Redeemer in the
catacombs

1

. . . .

THE MYTH OF ITS ORIGINS,
THE ORIGIN OF ITS MYTHS

Several self-serving myths, put about by Fritz Lang and his company, the
Universum Film Aktiengesellschaft (UFA), hang over *Metropolis*. The
myth-making started with the story of how the film came to be
conceived: in October 1924, Fritz Lang and his producer Erich Pommer
travelled to New York, for the US opening of *Siegfried's Death*, the first
part of *Die Nibelungen*, the four-hour disaster spectacle depicting the
heroic origins of the Germanic nation out of 'hate, murder and revenge'.
Because of visa difficulties, the two visitors had to stay on board the 'SS
Deutschland'for an extra night before being allowed to disembark. In the
evening, Lang and Pommer went on deck to see the Manhattan skyline
for the first time. An idea was born:

> I saw a street, lit as if in full daylight by neon lights and topping them,
> oversized luminous, advertising moving turning flashing on and off,
> spiralling [...] something which was completely new and near fairy-
> tale like for a European in those days, and this impression gave me the
> first thought of an idea for a town of the future.[1]

But by October 1924, the concept for *Metropolis* had been in Thea von
Harbou's and Fritz Lang's minds for nearly a year. Pommer had publicly

mentioned it after the Berlin premiere of *Die Nibelungen* in January 1924, Erich Kettelhut, the art director, had seen a version of the script around May 1924, and a Viennese paper had quoted Thea von Harbou working on 'the screenplay for their new film *Metropolis*' in July 1924. Of course, the script and the film (and the novel and the film) are two different things: the discrepancy between the story and its style has itself been one of the founding oppositions securing much mythic potency for the finished film. Nevertheless, several pieces of (film-) history hide inside this story of the Manhattan skyline as the origin of *Metropolis*.

The Parufamet Agreement

The trip to the US in late 1924 by Pommer and Lang was indeed crucial for the origin of *Metropolis*, though more decisive than New York was the subsequent stop in Los Angeles. It made the two most famous men of the German cinema realise why the gap had become so wide between the Europeans and Hollywood, and what obstacles lay in the way of UFA films penetrating the US market. They visited the production facilities of the major studios, they saw the latest film-making technology, they talked not only to executives like Joseph Schenk, Sam Goldwyn and Marcus Loew, but also to directors and actors like Chaplin, Thomas Ince and Mary Pickford. Lang met up again with Ernst Lubitsch, who had made Hollywood his home in 1921, and Douglas Fairbanks told Lang that German films would not sell in America until UFA put more effort into launching its players as internationally recognised stars.[2] Pommer in the meantime was shopping for two Mitchell cameras which were among the

Pommer and Lang, embarked for New York, 1924 (Stiftung Deutsche Kinemathek Berlin)

four used for shooting *Metropolis* (the other two were a French Debrie, the standard studio-camera and a German Stachow, the latter more robust, suitable for Günther Rittau's special effects). On his way back, Lang also visited D. W. Griffith who had just finished making *Isn't Life Wonderful* (1924), set (but not shot) in a wintry and hungry post-war Germany, much to the visible irritation of Lang, who probably fancied himself sole owner of the image-bank 'Germany'.

Other reasons for the US visit had to do with UFA's parlous state. The German film industry was in crisis. Its blossoming in the early 20s proved short-lived, based as it was on exploiting the trading advantages of a rapidly depreciating currency, which allowed German firms to export their films below cost. After the stabilisation of the Reichsmark in 1924, it was the Americans' turn to do the 'dumping' on the German market with productions that had already returned their investment in the huge domestic market. Pommer knew that his films had to draw level with the Americans as far as production values were concerned, if UFA were to retain even its share of the German box-office. But with increased budgets came the need to make films for export. The success in France of *Die Nibelungen* had raised hopes that this might be the breakthrough film in the US as well. Pommer was talking in New York and Los Angeles about a distribution deal, where US Majors would import ten UFA films per annum, in exchange for UFA's first-run houses show-casing twenty American films. The Americans were seriously concerned about maintaining open access to the lucrative German market, the German film industry having successfully lobbied parliament to introduce import restrictions in 1924. After almost a year of negotiations and near-misses, the US Major–UFA deal was finally sealed in December 1925. Known as the Parufamet Agreement (after the three companies involved: Famous-Players-Lasky through their distribution arm *Par*amount , *UFA* and the *Met*ro-Goldwyn-Mayer Corporation), it proved for UFA a Trojan horse as well as a poisoned chalice. In exchange for a US $4 million (16.8 million Reichsmark) loan, UFA agreed to reserve up to 75 per cent of the bookings in its 135 first-run cinemas for its US partners. They, in turn, arguing that the American public was volatile in its tastes, reserved the right to decide where, how and which UFA films to show in their theatres.

Some of the troubles that were to make *Metropolis* a notorious case (and casualty) are probably attributable to the Parufament Agreement, under whose terms it was one of the first major productions. It explains, for instance, the supposed profligacy of Lang and the open-ended sums he seems to have had at his disposal. To Pommer, his *carte blanche* for Lang was justified in view of the prize to be bagged, the prospect of a major hit in the US. But just how big a risk UFA's star producer was taking can be seen when the figures are put in perspective. The company's net profits in 1924–5 were 3.1 million Reichmark; at that time, the average production cost of a feature film was 175,000 Reichmark. *Metropolis* was originally budgeted for 800,000 Reichmark, but its final bill – UFA argued, but Lang disputed – was nearer 4.2 million Reichmark, half of the entire production budget of 1925–6. The rest had to be spread across the other twenty-two films made that season.[3] The gamble cost Pommer his neck, and already in January 1926, long before the film was finished, he had exchanged his place on the UFA board for a producer's office at Famous-Players-Lasky, no doubt a move also facilitated by the visit in 1924.

Thea von Harbou

Back in Berlin, Thea von Harbou was also working on *Metropolis*. Besides being Lang's wife, a celebrated novelist in her own right and UFA's top screenwriter, Harbou was a contract writer for the Scherl-Verlag, one of Berlin's three publishing empires, owned and controlled by press-tsar and ultra-conservative would-be politician Alfred Hugenberg. For Harbou, both *Die Nibelungen* and *Metropolis* were book tie-ins, a practice UFA had pursued with Fritz Lang films since *Dr Mabuse* (loosely based on Norbert Jacques's serialised novel, published by the rival Ullstein Verlag). Most likely, while Lang was in America, von Harbou was writing the novel rather than working on the screenplay. However, there is room for doubt which came first, or rather, how many different versions of each she was working on at any one time.[4]

Metropolis was serialised in *Das illustrierte Blatt* from August 1926 onwards, six months prior to the film's premiere.[5] But correspondence dated 22 February 1926 indicates that the Scherl desk editor asked von Harbou to tone down the film references in the story and rewrite the material more like a self-contained novel. What is also on record is that throughout 1924, von Harbou was busy reading herself into the literature of futuristic civilisations: two French novels and one English were consulted, Jules Verne's *The Five Hundred Millions of the Begum*, Claude Farrère's *Les Condamnés à mort* and H. G. Wells' *When the*

Sleeper Wakens. Nearer home, Georg Kaiser's theatre trilogy *Koralle*, *Gas I* and *Gas II*, Ernst Toller's play about a failed worker's revolution, *Maschinenstürmer*, Ernst Ludwig's *Zwischen Himmel und Erde* (for the showdown on the Cathedral roof-top), Max Reinhardt's and Hugo von Hofmannsthal's *Das Große Welt-Theater* (for the macabre Cathedral 'Dance of Death'), and another play by the mid-nineteenth-century playwright C. D. Grabbe were also within reach. She was nothing if not thorough, employing a permanent personal secretary-typist, to whom she dictated scenes or chapters, usually while knitting to maintain concentration.[6]

Von Harbou's novel and the film-script differ in many respects.[7] But given that the shooting script has not survived, and that the film as it has come down poses enough textual and editorial conundrums of its own, attempts to pin down exactly the relation between the two were for a long time little more than guess-work or intertextual inference, often ending up by ridiculing von Harbou for her appalling prose.[8] Today the novel is indeed almost unreadable, yet it perfectly blended Expressionist pathos with the mass-circulation formulas of the time, in its genre of bestselling awfulness no different from other (male and female) popular novelists such as Karl May, Norbert Jacques, Charlotte Birch-Pfeiffer or Hedwig Courts-Mahler.

Preceded by the motto: 'This book is an event braiding itself around the insight that the mediator between brain and hands has to be the heart' and dedicated to 'Friedel' (Fritz Lang), the novel opens with Freder, the son of the master of Metropolis, playing the organ in his studio. Floods of tears are streaming down his face as he re-lives the scene of his first meeting with Maria, the simple woman of the people. Over long periods in the novel the perspective is that of Freder, since the story casts him as a reluctant saviour, realising eventually that his task was not only to 'mediate' between brain and hand in the social conflict of management and labour, but to redeem the soul of his hard-hearted father Joh Fredersen by reconciling him to the loss of his wife Hel during childbirth. Expressionist also by virtue of its theme of redemption, the novel blends two Western archetypes, the seeker-hero Oedipus, and the sacrificial hero Jesus and the Pietà. The matriarchal story-line runs from Maria to Hel to Joh's mother, and crosses the patriarchal story-line of two rivals in mortal combat over the possession of a woman. Quite logically, therefore, the novel does not end on the couple Maria and Freder, or the handshake between foreman and boss, but with Joh Fredersen visiting his aged mother who hands him a letter written by his wife on her death-bed, confirming that it was Joh she loved, not his rival Rotwang.

In 1979, the Stiftung Deutsche Kinemathek in Berlin acquired from the estate of Gottfried Huppertz, Lang's composer for both *Die Nibelungen* and *Metropolis*, an early version of the script of *Metropolis*, and a more thorough comparison between novel and screenplay became possible. Though not the shooting script, Huppertz' copy proved an invaluable find: it gave subsequent restoration work on the film one of the much-needed breakthroughs. But the Huppertz script also casts light on the Lang/von Harbou collaboration from script to film and back to the published novel. By comparing scenes in this script with various published extracts from Lang's shooting script, one can follow Lang at work. These divergent sources – all of which bear her signature – suggest that von Harbou was indeed a multi-talent, able to work to different specifications as well as for different media and audiences: her authorship lay in her utter lack of originality when it came to the verbal and visual clichés by which she shaped her none the less unique vision.

Lang and von Harbou: Siamese Twins?
Metropolis's literary and stage sources were immediately identified.[9] Kurt Pinthus, in his opening-night review, named most of them and concluded his summary by throwing up his hands in mock-despair: 'To discuss the ridiculousness of the story-line linking all these motifs is already to overestimate it. To remain silent is in this case the highest respect one can pay the lady in question.'[10] Other critics followed suit.[11] Rubbing it in most mercilessly was the young Luis Buñuel, writing in Madrid's *La Gaceta Literaria*:

> *Metropolis* is not one film, *Metropolis* is two films joined by the belly, but with divergent, indeed extremely antagonistic, spiritual needs. Those who consider the cinema as a discreet teller of tales will suffer a profound disillusion with *Metropolis*. What it tells us is trivial, pretentious, pedantic, hackneyed romanticism. But if we put before the story the plastic-photogenic basis of the film, then *Metropolis* will come up to any standards, will overwhelm us as the most marvellous picture book imaginable […]. Even though we must admit that Fritz Lang is an accomplice, we hereby denounce as the presumed author of

these [i.e. *Der müde Tod* and *Metropolis*] eclectic essays and of this hazardous syncretism his wife, the scenarist Thea von Harbou.[12]

French critics divided the film's merits in roughly the same way.[13] *Les Annales* called Lang 'a lyricist, capable of extraordinary images and imagination', but when left to his own devices, a mere child:

> [from the *metteur en scène* of *Die Nibelungen*] one expects grandeur, intelligence and poetry, but [in *Metropolis*] one only finds ponderousness, pretension and puerility. The script of *Metropolis* is of unsurpassable stupidity. One suspects a con-trick: a schoolboy's badly executed homework is somehow taken seriously, the dreams of [A.] Tolstoi, Villiers de l'Isle Adam and [H. G.] Wells are tossed together like a salad by the family idiot.[14]

This Manichaean division of labour between husband and wife, however, must be considered another of the founding myths of *Metropolis*, its credibility strengthened by the two protagonists' subsequent careers, when von Harbou and Lang became estranged, went their separate ways and von Harbou joined the Nazi Party. Lang sometimes seemed to agree with Buñuel, though more often apologising on his own behalf rather than blaming his ex-wife for the sentimental naïvety of *Metropolis*'s social message.[15] But seeing how they continued working together and even lived in the same apartment until Lang left for France in 1933, the shared secret of their – uniquely successful – collaboration must have been a bond beyond politics or marital infidelities.[16]

The intervening decades, and a different appreciation of mainstream film-making, have helped to upgrade one's respect for von Harbou's synthetic imagination. Among the reasons that make *Metropolis* a classic are surely its cultural hybridity and insouciant mingling of high sentiment and low cunning in threading so many archetypal situations into one multi-strand story-line, creating characters that never pretend to an individualised psychology and who are none the less unforgettable. Hidden in von Harbou's story are references to Eastern, Egyptian, Judeo-Christian, Greek and cabbalist traditions of esoteric thought, and Lang's designs resonate with the knowing echoes of so many icons of avant-garde visual culture that the incoherences act more like cognitive jolts or musical dissonances. The musical analogy was intended: the script consists of 406 tableaux, each with its own heading. They are in turn grouped into three 'movements' of uneven length, with part one ('Prelude') comprising 155 tableaux, part two ('Intermezzo') taking us from tableau 156 to 224, and part three ('Furioso') making up the final 181 tableaux.

Metropolis's incoherence is thus a matter of perspective. One of the objections in 1927 was that the film pretended to be about the future, when in fact it made no plausible predictions, either regarding technological advances or social life in the era of mass civilisation.[17] But since nothing ages more quickly than imagined futures, the appeal of science fiction lies rarely in its predictive power. *Metropolis* is no exception, and in its slant on the present it does have documentary value.[18] The story can be read as a compendium text of topical material, lifting motifs from Christian mythology and German Romantic fairy-tales, in order to graft them onto its dystopic urban parable.[19] Critics quickly picked up on architectural debates and housing issues, labour laws and film politics. Despite its lack of realism, the film is something of a psychogram or fever-chart of the late 20s which across its tale of technology run riot and industrial regimentation, is obsessed with rising temperatures, pressures coming to a head, bubbling liquids on the boil, imminent explosions and inundating floods: in short, it records all manner of forces welling up from the deep.[20] It also opposes to America's perceived optimism of unlimited progress and Fordist pragmatism the self-consciously European clamour for spiritual values, embodied in Weimar Germany's defensively hesitant, sentimentally pessimist, but also stoical or even cynical takes on modernity. Theodor Heuss (later to become the first President of the Federal Republic in 1948) noted that in its *mélange* of Christian symbols, archaic motifs and sub-literary stereotypes *Metropolis* illustrated 'the cramped spiritual atmosphere of our age, when the banal is blown up to heroic dimensions, the heroic is transformed into mysticism, and the mysticism is passed off as tragedy'.[21] Yet although it may take the moral(ising) high-ground, Lang/von Harbou's film is none the less rife with anxiety, which at the depth-psychological or fantasy level makes *Metropolis* all-too-coherent, a fact not always recognised at the time, but one of the key points brought out by structuralist and feminist critics in the 80s, when *Metropolis* once more returned to prominence. The director set out to create a populist idiom for his vision of modernity, rather than following the avant-garde and deploying the film-language of Eisenstein, Pudovkin or Ruttmann, certainly well known to Lang. That the finished film failed to ignite – or even reach – most of the audience it was intended for, heightens its interest as a film-political document, but does not in itself invalidate the try. For if critics at the time thought the stylistic clashes and the commercial calculations offensive, it was not only because they expected a 'realistic' version of the future. The misunderstanding extended to the belief that a film could only be art and thus something of value if it were an original and organic work, all of one piece. *Metropolis*, however, positioned itself explicitly as a quite different experience: not a palimpsest, more like a dream-screen or a polished reflector, where the very absence of psychologically detailed characters, exacerbated by Lang's complex editing, gave a somnambulist ambiguity of motivation to the protagonists' gestures and a hovering indeterminacy to their actions, perhaps too quickly derided as the director's 'well-known' inability to handle actors.[22] His tableau-style may have inhibited viewer identification and irritated adherents of montage-kino and the recently imported *Russenfilme*, but it powerfully fed into a peculiar kind of poetry, attractive to some (such as Buñuel), repellent to many others. Such high-tech/low-culture eclecticism, at any rate, became a mainstream movie idiom *par excellence* and one compelling reason for cinema's general impact on the arts of the twentieth century.

Metropolis's combination of sophisticated design with the radical naïvety of mythic clichés in the mode of a self-referential *mise en abyme* is now a familiar feature of mainstream film-making, almost a condition for entering the international market in the first place. Like Steven Spielberg's 'politically correct' (i.e. timid) fairy-tales or George Lucas's *Star Wars* saga, Lang and von Harbou's film shows the 'imagineer' at work, rather than the artist striving for self-expression. Also comparable to Spielberg and Lucas, there was in von Harbou and Lang a didactic streak, a belief in the cinema educating the child in all of us: making the message pristine, but overwhelming the senses in order to touch core (at times, atavistic) emotions.

Alphabet Soup of the Avant-garde

Tracking down von Harbou's sources and Lang's borrowings would thus miss the target if it were done in a spirit to convict them of plagiarising or even trivialising the fine arts and literature, since the point of this

Stalactites
supporting the
Eternal Gardens in
Metropolis (top)
and Alberich's cave
in *Siegfried's
Death* (Heidi
Schönemann,
Potsdam)

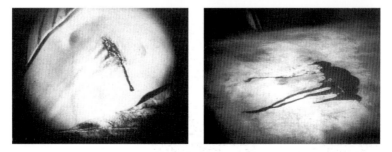

Blood and water: the Dragon's fatal wound in *Siegfried's Death* (left) and the City's fatal
wound in *Metropolis* (Stadtmuseum-Filmmuseum, Munich)

Walter Schulze-Mittendorf, Head of Machine
Maria, 1926 (above). Oskar Schlemmer, *Mask
in Yellow and Black*, 1923 (Schönemann).

Kurt Schmidt, *Man at the
Control-console*, 1924
(Schönemann). Freder
crucified at the controls
(bottom).

19

international superproduction was to create a work with a recognition factor that made contact with different kinds of cultural memory as well as stir deep-rooted fantasies, while setting out to provide an experience where the eye perceives what the mind can only marvel at. In its cultural memory, the film is a sponge, soaking up as much ideological and somatic material as the disaster of the First World War and its political aftermath – the failed revolution on the left and the resentment of an unjust peace on the right – had left behind as debris and ferment. Therefore, the fantasies had to be millennial and apocalyptic: Joh Fredersen's guilt and conversion, his son Freder's eye-witness accounts of dehumanisation and destruction and Maria's self-sacrifice are key features of the plot. These redemptive yearnings had been prominent in the Expressionist literature and had fuelled the utopian revolutionary politics of the earlier part of the decade.

In its iconography, too, *Metropolis* is a subtly knowing film, as *Zeitgeist*-conscious as *haute couture* and bestseller *belles-lettres*. Leaving aside for a moment the architectural designs and their pedigree, the wealth of direct references to the visual arts, paintings, graphics, sculpture, museum pieces, fashion accessories, book-design and commercial art is astonishing. Several Berlin reviewers commented in shocked (or mock-shocked) recognition on Freder reading in his sick-bed a copy of the *Book of Revelations*, recently published by the fashionably esoteric Avalun Verlag Hellerau (the shot has since disappeared from the prints).[23] They also spotted references to now near-forgotten Expressionist artists such as Karl Völker and Hans Hoerle. Lotte Eisner has tracked down some of the theatre echoes in her *Haunted Screen*, referring to Max Reinhardt for the crowd-scenes, and Erwin Piscator's *Sprech-Chöre* as precursors of all those extras raising their hands in staggered supplication. She also mentions filmic citations, such as Otto Rippert's 1916 *Homunculus* and the French avant-garde, yet Lang makes references to own films. The underground stalactites of Alberich's cave in *Die Nibelungen* turn up again in the 'Eternal Gardens'. Both were modelled on Hans Pölzig's columns in the 'Große Schauspielhaus' Berlin, too well known for reviewers to even bother to point them out. The fuming cauldron of jewels from which the false Maria rises is supported by kneeling black slaves exactly the way the chest containing the Treasure of the Nibelungen was supported by stone dwarfs come to life in *Siegfried's Death*. The water breaking through the concrete floor of the underground city is shot like the blood gushing from the Dragon's mortal wound, and many of the crowd-and-disaster scenes are reprises from *Kriemhild's Revenge*. When Heidi Schönemann began seriously researching Lang's films for their art-historical references, she discovered models even for such apparently trivial accessories as the glass statue adorning Joh Fredersen's office coffee table (based on a design by Peter Behrens). Equally surprising, she found a constructivist drawing (by Karl Schmidt) that had clearly inspired the kitsch-Expressionist crucifixion scene at the dial controls, and the image that stood as model for Walter Schulze-Mittendorf's design of the robot-mask combines a drawing for a ballet by Oskar Schlemmer with a bronze head by Rudolf Belling (there also exists a still showing Lang and Karl Freund fitting the guards of Moloch with a West African mask, probably from the Berlin Völkerkundliche Museum, a favourite haunt of Expressionists like Schmidt-Rottluff, Kirchner and Haeckel). The 'Eternal Gardens' resemble a Jugendstil magazine cover by Fido from 1909, and another critic thought he spotted a painting by one Gert Wollheim, adding sarcastically 'held in the collection of the Prussian State'.[24] Some of Änne Willkomm's costumes for the ladies of the night are taken from a Bauhaus collection by Schlemmer, and finally, Rotwang's gingerbread house, rather than a pure Gothic fantasy, is modelled after a villa built by the Expressionist architect Otto Bartning for the director of a Saxony steel works between 1923 and 1925, itself probably based on an illustration first published in 1905 by Julius Dietz, who just happens to have been Lang's drawing teacher in Munich.[25]

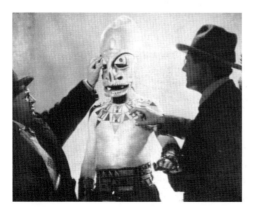

Freund and Lang with West African mask

Rotwang's gothic golem house among the high-rises (Schönemann)

These avant-garde accents from the contemporary fine and applied arts confirm just how conscious the makers of *Metropolis* were of their attempt to build on previous Pommer export successes such as *The Cabinet of Dr Caligari* (1920), and how deliberately they set about pioneering a recognisably German prototype of a 'designer-blockbusters'. Though its

disappointing box-office and Pommer's departure for the US meant that the prototype never went into serial production, it needs to be stressed that the impact of *Metropolis* in 1927 was enormous: hardly an article in the papers that year did not make reference to it, including a fair number of cartoons and parodies. In what sense can one therefore say that Lang, von Harbou and UFA did not succeed? Even if this is the case from the financial point of view, the reasons were not necessarily aesthetic, as critics averred: they were as much due to bad luck or bad timing, and they pinpoint the risks always carried by prototypes.

Otto Bartning, Director's villa, Zeipau, 1923–5 (Schönemann)

2
. . . .
THE UFA-CREW

The Cathedral Master Builders
Shooting started on 22 May 1925 and went on until 30 October 1926, clocking up 310 working days (and sixty nights). In principle, it should not have been such a Herculean task. To meet the technical challenges, Lang could rely on his proven *Nibelungen* team, headed by Otto Hunte as chief architect, whose most gifted junior partner was Erich Kettelhut.[26]

Th. Heine, 'The Recipe for Metropolis', from *Simpl*, February 1926: 'take ten tons of horror ... pour on 10% sentimentality ... bring it to the boil with social conscience ... and season to taste with mysticism ... finally, stir the whole with marks (several millions) ... and ready is your mega-picture'

Freund and Lang, with the crew knee-deep in water (Stiftung Deutsche Kinemathek Berlin)

Also on hand from *Die Nibelungen* was Karl Vollbrecht and for the costumes, Änne Willkomm, apparently much abused by Lang and later to marry Kettelhut. The cameraman this time was Karl Freund, a regular from F. W. Murnau's crew, with Günther Rittau, by then UFA's acknowledged expert for some of the most intricate in-camera trick

effects, who on *Die Nibelungen* had assisted Carl Hoffmann. Lang himself was no novice with special effects, either in-camera, or on a large-scale purpose-built set. The miniaturised marching armies and the self-scrolling letter in *Der müde Tod* (1921) were partly Lang's own invention, and the dragon in *Siegfried's Death* (1923) was an engineering feat admired even by Willis O'Brien, the special effects expert whom Lang had visited on the set of *The Lost World* (after Arthur Conan Doyle) at First National during his US trip. This time, the task was not only to create mechanical monsters, like the Moloch-machine or Rotwang's lab which was to inspire a dozen Boris Karloff and Bela Lugosi pictures. The real difficulties came with the architectural scale models, many of which were designed by Kettelhut, who has left a detailed account of the shoot in his (unpublished) memoirs.[27] Vistas and perspectives, surging crowds, collapsing buildings and wrecked machinery had to be stitched and segued into real live action, set in a throbbing city and planned in dimensions that only existed in the mind. It called for a special kind of imagination for these bodies in space, scale models, back-projection, mirror-shots and stop-frame animation to meld and blend together, as literally hundreds of automobiles, aeroplanes, human beings and other moving parts had to be fitted together. Rittau, too, has written an account of some of the effects, such as the animation of the traffic in the exterior shots, the explosion in the machine room, the flooding of the underground city and the metamorphosis of the robot into the likeness of Maria:

> Electric current tends to be invisible. On the other hand, the phantastic-mysterious transformation now taking place naturally had to be rendered in images. We illuminated liquids in strange test-tubes and made them bubble, the electric apparatus surrounding Maria was made to emit sparks and we gradually enveloped it in huge arcs of lightning, at the same time as rings of fire formed around the robot, moving up and down her body. As she became human, her blood circulation lit up. We spent months in the lab preparing these effects, with photo-chemistry playing a major role, as well as the most unlikely aids [... such as] a silver ball, black velvet, liquid soap, vaseline, vignettes [...]. Some strips of celluloid had to be exposed up to thirty times.[28]

The process-shots of the stadium and the Tower of Babel were largely given over to Eugen Shüfftan, who was to make his reputation with *Metropolis* by developing a special matte-shot device by partially scraping the tain off a mirror through which an action could be filmed, while a painted backdrop or scenery was reflected back into the image. Several street scenes, the interiors of the Cathedral, Freder's horror vision of the Moloch machine were all done using the Schüfftan-process. Built scale models of the heart-machine allowed the simulation of an explosion: according to Rittau, forty metres of film took eight days'

work, for ten seconds of screen time. The initial explosion witnessed by
Freder took four weeks to prepare and less than two minutes to shoot.
Each of the many other spectacular scenes – from the underground
inundation to the shaven-headed slaves building the Tower of Babel or
the burning of the false Maria on the stake – also consumed weeks and
months, clocking up production costs, causing frayed tempers, walk-outs
and hours of merciless rehearsal time often in freezing conditions.[29] One
of the actors in the inundation scene caught pneumonia after standing,
day in day out, for hours in the water and irreparably damaged his voice:
he was still telling this story to anyone willing to listen as late as 1939 in his
Paris exile.

The seventeen-year-old, inexperienced Brigitte Helm, pushed by
an ambitious mother, had to be groomed for a demanding double role:
Maria the Virgin Mary, mother-figure and herald of the world's saviour;
and Maria the robot, extra-terrestrial, *femme fatale* and she-devil
incarnate. Some of the most taxing tasks turned out to be the endless
hours spent on the robot scenes, surprisingly brief in the finished film, but
dreadfully long in preparing the (wooden) casing and make-up. In other

scenes, such as the burning
at the stake (with real
flames), or the chase by
Rotwang up the Cathedral
tower, where at one point
Maria swings helplessly
from a bell-rope before
Rotwang roughly hauls her
over an iron railing, one
can almost smell the seared
clothes and feel the metal
bruise her legs. Gustav
Fröhlich, by contrast, was
not Lang's first choice and
was only picked from
among the extras after the
first lead had stormed off
the set, necessitating re-
shoots.[30] Even at the time,
his acting was severely

Maria swinging from the bell-rope

criticised as relentlessly over-emphatic, without nuance or modulation between horror and ecstasy, as he impulsively charges forward or recoils in nameless terror.

Metropolis illustrates the UFA style at its best and worst. The no-expenses-spared attention to detail, the time taken for rehearsals and preparation, the armies of assistants, hopeful actors and patient extras all gave the director an unprecedented freedom, but also a huge responsibility. While the script was worked out down to the minutiae of lighting, blocking and camera-movements, it seems there was also room for trial-and-error experiments on the set. Von Harbou, for instance, was at the director's side throughout, no doubt also in her capacity as screenwriter. Telling in this respect are the precise annotations about costume, camera positions and technical sketches on the margins of the (lost) shooting script, of which several pages were reproduced in the special *Ufa Magazin* and other pre-screening publications.[31] The director-unit system, such as Pommer allowed for his two stars Lang and Murnau – each with an experienced and extensive crew allocated to a single project that might last a small eternity – did not give the studio the sort of control over production schedules and cost-overruns that managers or accountants like to have.[32] The up-side was that this team-spirit allowed for sustained creative input from a wide array of top professionals: to live with *Metropolis* for nearly two years must have generated its own kind of intensity. As Lotte Eisner pointed out in *The Haunted Screen*, the sense of a coherent (misleadingly called 'Expressionist') style for the classic 20s German cinema was due in large

Lang, Helm and von Harbou making music

part to the close co-operation between set designers, cameramen, art directors and countless other, highly skilled specialists who had made a successful transition from designer and decorator work in the theatre to the cinema. Yet unlike the US Majors with which it was competing, UFA did not run a big special effects department. In the spirit of the medieval master builders, the studio hired these different experts on a project-by-project basis.[33] Often, they brought with them not only their own equipment and assistants, but also their trade secrets.[34] This did not stop the UFA publicity department bragging about the technical brilliance of its craftsmen in fan magazines and special editions of the house journal, *Ufa Magazin*.[35]

What was new about the making of *Metropolis* – and another lesson possibly picked up from the Pommer/Lang US trip – was the extensive pre-screening publicity, the work-in-progress reports, the constant leaking to the press of stories, the arranged interviews and on-set visits. Throughout the nearly eighteen-month period the papers were full of production reports. Scarcely a week went by without the trade journals like the *Licht-Bild-Bühne* or the *Film-Kurier* reporting on major developments or setbacks. Journalists were falling over each other to file stories about the shooting of the film. Billy Wilder claims to have watched Lang at work, as did Curt Siodmak.[36] Hitchcock is known to have visited the set, though hardly as the major director he was yet to become. Eisenstein let himself be photographed with Lang and the *Metropolis* crew, as did other national and international celebrities. In Berlin in 1925, it was a sign of belonging to the smartest in-crowd to have seen Lang and von Harbou at work. They were featured at home, posing

Director, actors, cameramen and crew posing for the family album

with pets, exotic artefacts and tasteful furnishings, in the illustrated press.
The horror stories about endless rehearsals, the inclemencies of the
weather, the superlatives about the number of extras (36,000 adults,[37] 750
children, 100 blacks), about the extravagance of the props (35,000 pairs of
shoes, seventy-five wigs, fifty specially-built automobiles) and other
material excesses (620,000 metres negative stock exposed) originated
from the UFA publicity department itself – only to be used afterwards as
a stick to beat the director with, for his profligacy, his sadism with actors
and his dictatorial capriciousness.[38]

The Opening Night
When the film eventually opened on 10 January 1927 at the UFA-Palast
am Zoo in Berlin, expectations had been raised to fever pitch. No less
than 1,200 spectators attended the premiere, including Reichskanzier
Wilhelm Marx, several cabinet ministers and deputies, foreign
ambassadors and even royalty.[39] The music was performed by a full
orchestra and directed by the composer, Gottfried Huppertz.
Subsequently published as a piano score for regional and smaller cinema
venues, it keeps a judicious balance between tonal pieces, in the manner
of late Romantic music, or transpositions of well-known melodies
(including the *Marseillaise*, when the workers are destroying the
machines), and a-tonal passages to indicate the modern rhythms of the
city, without, however, venturing as far as Edmund Meisel was to do, in
his scores for Eisenstein's *Battleship Potemkin* or Ruttmann's *Berlin –
Symphony of a City*. There was even a set of gramophone records of the
orchestral arrangement, with a spoken introduction to the film by Lang
himself.[40] The gala brochure, put together by UFA publicist Stefan
Lorant, was an instant collector's item. The novel was presented to
invited guests in a pig-skin bound edition which, as Siegfried Kracauer
sarcastically remarked on a similar occasion the year after, filled the
auditorium with its own kind of aroma.[41] The UFA publicity machine
had made sure that the opening was as perfectly choreographed as 'the
making of *Metropolis*' had been designed as if it were an election
campaign.[42] At a running time of almost three hours, there was a break
during which, as one critic remarked, it became already clear that the
reviews would be divided. At the end of the gala evening, there were
standing ovations for all the major players, the director and von Harbou.
As Kettelhut noted: at the party for the cast and crew, 'a spirit of universal

brotherhood reigned supreme', obviously alluding ironically to the moral of the film itself. But in the press the next day, a distinct sense of disappointment: maybe UFA had placed too much hope in its own hype and the oversell had taken its toll. Not even this extraordinary film, it seems, could compete with its own publicity.[43]

3

....

A RUIN-IN-PROGRESS:
RELEASE VERSIONS AND RESTORATIONS

The Three Release Versions
The film shown to the gala audience had been passed by the censorship board on 13 November 1926 at a length of 4,189 metres. The day after the premiere, it transferred for four months to the UFA-Pavilion at the Nollendorfplatz, and briefly opened in Vienna (10 February 1927).[44] Already in December 1926 another negative had been taken to the US by Frederick Wynne-Jones, UFA's US representative, for the New York release. The Paramount executives were not impressed: for a film without stars and a story-line they could not follow they refused a special show-case. At two-and-a-half-hours screening time, *Metropolis* did not fit the normal exhibition schedule, and the decision was taken to cut it to one-and-three-quarter-hours (i.e. from twelve reels to the standard seven-reel feature). The playwright Channing Pollock was hired to rewrite the continuity and titles. Pollock and Paramount produced two (near-identical) versions: one for the US market and one for Britain and the Commonwealth.[45] On 7 March, *Metropolis* opened in New York, at the Rialto, at a length of 3,100 metres, shortened by a quarter. The London premiere was on 21 March at the Marble Arch Pavilion.[46] The story-line now concentrated on the relationship of Freder–Maria, with little to explain the rivalry between Joh Fredersen and Rotwang. The reason given for cutting out any mention of their common love, Hel, was that the name was too close to the English 'hell' and might give rise to guffaws. Also missing was most of the sub-plot involving Freder's helpers and minders: Josephat, Georgy and 'Slim', and therefore the surveillance and solidarity themes, no doubt close to Lang's heart, when one considers his previous and subsequent work. The depictions of the underground flood and the final chase were trimmed in length and

E. McKnight-Kauffer, art-deco
poster for British release,
London 1926 (Museum of
Modern Art, New York)

ferocity. Pollock defended his decisions vigorously: 'As it stood when I began my job of structural editing, *Metropolis* had no restraint or logic. It was symbolism run such riot that people who saw it couldn't tell what the picture was all about. I have given it my meaning.'[47]

In Berlin, the box-office was disappointing and the UFA board decided to pull the film in April, nervously looking to New York and halting all plans for a general release elsewhere in Germany.[48] On 5 August 1927, UFA resubmitted a version of 3,241 metres (slightly longer than the American version) to the Censorship Board, which went on general release on 26 August 1927. Thus already by August 1927, one had to distinguish three separate films: the first German release version, seen on the opening night and for a few weeks in Berlin, but then withdrawn. Depending on projection speed, it ran for between 160 and 205 minutes. Second, the American release version, most likely cut from a second print and shipped to Paramount, re-edited by Channing Pollock. His friend Randolph Bartlett explained the reasons for so drastically altering the film, downplaying the most obvious one, the fact that its length did not fit the standard schedule, and claiming that the film was 'now nearer Fritz Lang's idea than the version he himself released in Germany'.[49] Finally, the second German release version, which more or less followed the American version for its cuts and story-line re-editing. The UFA editors probably did not involve Lang, whose next project, a film based on episodes from the Bible, had been vetoed by the UFA board, whereupon Lang founded his own production company, henceforth using UFA merely as distributor.[50] *Metropolis*'s intertitles were altered once more (of the originally 175 intertitles thirty-six were eliminated and forty-five were rewritten) and some scenes were rearranged. Possibly for reasons of cost and time pressure, UFA cut the general release version from its original negative and appears to have neglected to preserve the cut material, more than 1,000 metres, containing several of the scenes most admired at the opening night.[51]

This is the more ironic, since another persistent myth about *Metropolis* has it that Lang shot huge amounts of footage: 620,000 metres negative and 1,300,000 metres positive film, amounting – for the first release version – to a staggering and highly improbable ratio of 148:1 for the negative. With such masses of footage, *Metropolis* must have been work-in-progress from the start: trimmed, cut and refitted like a suit on a tailor's dummy until it found the mass public it was made for. This apparent madness had some method and was not entirely unusual. Abel Gance's *Napoléon* (1926), for instance, is another famous film which from its inception existed in different release versions.[52] For *Metropolis*, the Parufamet Agreement also implied that the export market was divided between the US territory and the rest of the world. Erich Kettelhut mentions in his unpublished memoirs that on *Metropolis* Lang usually made sure he had at least three perfect takes of each scene. Was this yet another sign of Lang's aristocratic extravagance and his notoriously relentless perfectionism? The explanation may be simpler: given the production's international scope, Lang had probably agreed to deliver three completed negatives, one for the domestic market, one for Paramount, and one for UFA's own export division. Shot either successively or with different cameras, the takes would not be identical. There could thus, strictly speaking, be no 'original' of *Metropolis*.[53]

On the other hand, most historians (and archivists) have argued that the Berlin premiere version must be considered the 'authentic original' (an auteurist argument which pits Lang the artist against the money-men, to be distinguished from the postmodern re-released 'director's cut' instigated by the money-men). The two other versions would then be the result of, respectively, cynically commercial calculations by the US distributor, and the knee-jerk panic by UFA management, presiding over a film company in deep trouble. But this view was not inevitable, not even in 1927. The well-known critic Roland Schacht, whose reviews of *Metropolis* contain the only detailed comparison between the first and the second German version we possess, had few qualms about the cuts. He objected to the industry practice of show-casing films in Berlin for the benefit of the critics, considering them in any case paid PR-hacks. A serious reviewer should see a film under normal viewing conditions with a paying public, preferably in the provinces: what he called the 'utility' version, i.e. the film experience as it was likely to live in the minds of the mass audience.

Schacht also offered reasons why he felt the cuts were not missed. The fact that the sub-plot involving 'Slim' as Freder's minder had been eliminated did, according to him, mitigate the 'gross banality of the common-and-garden variety detective story', even if it made certain plot-points harder to follow. His comment on the removal of Hel is terse: 'a piece of mysticism that was as improbable as it left me indifferent.' His only note of regret has to do with sex and violence, because Schacht missed the lasciviousness and seductive nudity of the false Maria's performance at Rotwang's home, as well as the brutal bouts of violence between the upper-class men at the Yoshiwara fighting over Brigitte Helm's garter. Another scene – to him 'one of the most amazing scenes of all contemporary cinema' – had also been cut: that of Georgy, the worker in Freder's clothes seeing (or fantasising) in the back of a motor-car that draws up next to him a semi-nude ('an Otto-Dix drawing come to life, incredibly sexual and ravishingly photographed'). But even in his review of the Berlin premiere, Schacht went so far as to implore Lang to cut the film to no more than two hours: if the director was not prepared to do it himself, he should let someone else perform this act of mercy.[54]

Schacht's account thus corroborates indirectly the closeness of the second German release version to the Paramount version(s), but his apparent indifference to the losses further deepens the puzzle of the status of the Berlin premiere version. Maybe this 'long' version was never

The Vamp to die for

intended to be the definitive film, but simply a deluxe 'performance' for the demanding metropolitan elite, the prototype of another familiar phenomenon today: a blockbuster's first-run in the cinema as the marketing ploy and publicity magnet to prepare video sales, TV screenings and other subsidiary and residual exploitations. That UFA did not have a chance to cash in on its own blockbuster may have had as its more contingent reason the ballyhoo created by the coming of sound in 1928, which made such typically and consummately 'silent' films as *Metropolis* (and G. W. Pabst's similarly ill-fated *Pandora's Box* [1928]) victims of bad timing and thus (temporarily) obsolete.[55] With the sound revolution, the film disappeared into limbo, only re-emerging with the renewed interest in movie blockbusters in the 1970s, accompanied as this was by the revival of 'silent classics' at film festivals such as Pordenone's Giornate del cinema muto. Kevin Brownlow and David Gill's spectacular reconstruction of *Napoléon* in the late 70s gave the Abel Gance blockbuster the Carl Davis and Carmine Coppola treatment, with live orchestra which in the age of pop concerts, stage musicals and rock operas has turned film screenings once more into a fond memory of the Wagnerian *Gesamtkunstwerk* film aesthetics once hoped the cinema would be heir to.

Either way, the fact is that after the first nine months of its life, *Metropolis* was a strange torso or changeling of a film, mutilated or merely mutated, depending on one's vantage point. No one exactly knows what the first-night audience saw, since neither von Harbou's script, nor the censorship cards give an accurate visual record of the actual film, however invaluable they and Huppertz' annotated score, with its 1,019 conductor's cues (of scene-changes and intertitles) proved to be as an aid to establishing the proper continuity of the action and the complicated alternations of Lang's original editing. Since the mid-80s, then, the combined efforts of scholars, collectors and archivists have progressively come closer to a kind of *Ur-text* also in respect of the visuals, mainly by minutely tracking the fate of the two remaining negatives and the myriad of 'generations' of prints struck from the Paramount versions and the second German release version.

Reconstructing a Classic: The Munich Version
Most of the copies of *Metropolis* in circulation until the 80s were taken from the second German release print of 1927, which as indicated, was

cut by more than a quarter, closely following the Paramount version. Its best available archive prints were those of the Museum of Modern Art, New York (2,532 metres, acquired in 1936 by Iris Barry on a visit to Berlin during the Olympic Games), of the National Film and TV Archive, London (which already in 1938 duped the New York print, but later found that it also held a damaged and incomplete British distribution copy of 2,602 metres), and a copy retained in the Reichsfilmarchiv Berlin (2,826 metres) removed by the Red Army in 1945 and deposited in the Gosfilmofond Archive Moscow.[56] The 35mm print re-certificated in 1962 in Germany by the post-war rights holders, the Friedrich Wilhelm Murnau Stiftung, was also based on the MoMA version. In the 60s, the Paramount version negative turned up in the State Film Archive of the GDR (East Berlin), having presumably been returned to Berlin by Paramount some time in the 30s after the original licence expired. Between 1969 and 1972 Eckart Jahnke at the GDR archive tried a first archival reconstruction, consulting the Paramount copy, but using the MoMA print owned by the NFTVA (2,927 metres) along with materials provided by other FIAF archives. Without the benefit of the Huppertz script, the censorship cards, or substantially new film material, this effort to reconstruct an authentic version remained largely conjecture, not least because Jahnke at the time seemed unaware of the history of the three release versions. Jahnke's reconstruction was, however, acquired by West German television (ZDF) and has frequently been shown (and widely circulates as an off-air recording in university film history classes).[57]

Reconstructing the 'original' *Metropolis* had always been high on any film archivist's wish list.[58] A kind of holy grail of the profession, it became a point of honour for one curator who dedicated a good deal of his professional life to it: Enno Patalas, from 1966 to 1995 director of the Munich Filmmuseum. In 1975, Patalas let it be known that he was actively working on restoring *Metropolis*, having already made his reputation with the restoration of other German film classics. In 1979, Gero Gandert, of the Stiftung Deutsche Kinemathek (West Berlin), bought the annotated copy of Thea von Harbou's script from Huppertz' widow. In 1980, the GDR archive discovered the November 1926 censorship record with the complete list of intertitles. In the meantime, Patalas had also learnt from Kenneth Anger about a private collector's print in Melbourne, Australia, but was unable to view a video of it until 1981, after the National Film and Sound Archive, Canberra had acquired the print from the collector's heirs. This was eventually identified as a copy of the British distribution print, but it contained scenes severely mutilated in all other prints, such as the stadium sequence near the opening, and equally exciting, it was colour-toned throughout: blue for night, sepia for interiors, dawn-grey for the final reconciliation in front of the Cathedral. In 1983, Patalas helped Giorgio Moroder with archival advice and, in exchange for tracking down the best preserved materials, Moroder financed a new print from the MoMA negative, of which Patalas received a copy. Also in 1983, Patalas looked at the three albums of production stills made by Horst von Harbou, Thea's brother. They had been donated in the mid-70s by Lang and Lily Latté to Henri Langlois of the Cinémathèque Française in Paris. While used for only two missing shots in the Munich version, the stills were more liberally interpolated in Moroder's version, to 'fill in' missing scenes of the 'Slim' plot-line. In 1987, the 'Munich' version (3,153 metres, edited by Gerhard Ullmann and Klaus Volkmer) had its premiere in Moscow, then subsequently in Munich, on both occasions with the original score by Huppertz, once

A triumph of design: the stadium as back projection mirror shot

Slim (Fritz Rasp) goes after Freder, but his plot-line stays on Paramount's cutting-room floor

arranged for piano, once with a full orchestra. This copy, although since shown all over the world, is not in general distribution, partly due to an unresolved rights question with the Murnau Stiftung, partly because the Munich Filmmuseum did not invest in a distribution copy, having always wanted first to restore the original intertitles and if possible, also the colour-toning. The Munich version is to date the philologically most accurate print of *Metropolis*, but as Patalas never omits to point out, it, too, is still a ruin-in-progress.[59]

Creating a Cult-Classic: The Moroder Version
These, broadly speaking, were the physical, but also film-historical conditions under which *Metropolis* existed when Moroder came on the scene in 1982. Apparently bidding against none other than David Bowie (with whom he had worked for Paul Schrader's remake of Jacques Tourneur's *Cat People* and who was also interested in doing something with *Metropolis*) Moroder acquired the rights from the Murnau Stiftung for a substantial sum. His 1984 re-issue can therefore be seen either as merely another business venture in the life-cycle of the film, or an adaptation, somewhere between a remake and a postmodern appropriation. Being a commercial proposition, it was not intended to compete with the Munich version, and yet, one might call it Lang's Last Laugh. First, because Moroder's version did find a mass-audience, helping *Metropolis* to metamorphose from the film history classic it had previously been, to the cult film classic it has since become. Second, because as already hinted at, *Metropolis* opened in New York barely three

months before *The Jazz Singer* (1927) had its premiere: it was probably drowned out elsewhere in the US in the din made by the coming of sound. Moroder, who made his reputation in the US both in the record business (he launched Donna Summers) and in movies (he won, among others, an Academy Award for the score of Alan Parker's *Midnight Express* [1978]), could justifiably claim that Lang did get a kind of revenge on Hollywood and sound: thanks to him, *Metropolis* finally had its proper American run, sixty-five years after its premiere.

The birth of *Metropolis* as cult film can thus be dated to the Cannes Film Festival of 1984, when this curious hybrid of archival restoration work, sacrilegious tampering with a venerated classic and an iconoclast pop-postmodern performance piece had its outing: that Moroder's version was newly minted, as it were, elicited nothing but gasps of joy among the assembled cinephiles, used to seeing a washed-out dupe even at the Paris Cinémathèque. That it was ruthlessly tinted and had the robot Maria lasciviously stripping to a disco beat must have been quite a shock to the devotees of Henry Langlois's Cathedral of the Seventh Art where pre-1928 films were always shown in silent gloom. As the *Nouvel Observateur* reported, mock-outraged, but also half in awed disbelief: 'Un rocker nommé Fritz Lang' was born.[60] Moroder's re-issue, at a cost of almost as much as UFA lost and with a New Wave soundtrack written by himself and performed by such chart-toppers as Freddy Mercury, Bonnie Tyler, Adam Ant and Pat Benatar, was bound to offend the purists if only because it smacked of such crass commercialism and seemed so evidently calculated to jump the culture barrier from 'art' to 'pop'.

According to his own account, Giorgio Moroder first had the idea of bringing *Metropolis* to a new audience back in 1980. Casting round for a suitable film he talked to Patalas who – quite generously, considering that he was himself working on an archival reconstruction – persuaded him to go for *Metropolis*. Moroder's solution to the problems of the archival reconstruction was to rely on his show-biz instincts. Using the MoMA print, i.e. the second German release version as backbone and skeleton, he fleshed it out with other bits he could lay his hands on. Occasionally he returned to the original intertitles for the censorship cards, rather than to Pollock's or UFA's doctored ones, or he inserted his own explanatory notes as narration over freeze-frames taken from the production stills of scenes presumed missing. More controversially, he

A Vision of Hel: Rotwang's monument to the woman he lost

printed dialogue titles as sub-titles rather than intertitles. Stills familiar from publicity material, posters and designs – a plunging view of the skyscrapers, the shell-shaped entrance to the Yoshiwara nightclub, Rotwang's memorial to the woman he lost to Fredersen – are also incorporated as establishing shots and linking sequences. The effect is to smooth transitions and to suggest a more precise (but also more limited) sense of location and action spaces for the narrative to circulate, cutting back and forth between them in a more conventional, classical Hollywood manner.

Moroder's *Metropolis*, down again to eighty-nine minutes is therefore not a cut version from an archive print but itself the result of re-editing. For those interested in the original and in the differences between German film-making and Hollywood in the 20s it is a fascinating document because it illustrates two distinct ways of thinking about film narrative. Narrative in Lang is generated not so much by the logic of the actions, but out of the *mise en scène* of part-objects, or rather, narrative is nothing other than an effect of the camera's ability to frame and reframe an object or scene and to displace itself in relation to that object or scene.[61]

This may seem like idle theorising, but it can also confirm that much of 20s German cinema was based on a visual grammar different from what we have come to accept as the norm, namely Hollywood-type continuity editing. Moroder gives the narrative a unilinear direction, via establishing shot, scene-dissection, close-up, by the simple expedient of relying on reverse-field editing and point-of-view shots to generate continuity, cutting out most of the inserts which in Lang's version had separated – in time and in space – the character's looks from their objects. To admirers of Lang, this is an unpardonable interference in the text, for the hallmark of his style is precisely the interpolation of disorienting or disrupting visuals into the classic match-cut sequence, making what is represented seem ambiguously motivated and always happening at one remove. In one of the linking sequences, for instance, Moroder reinstates something of the story of Georgy, the errant worker led astray in Yoshiwara, by zooming in and out of a still photograph, the staple technique of television documentaries when enlivening a static image by means of a rostrum camera. If we know that what Georgy would have stared at was the semi-nude of Schacht's description, then the zoom takes on an added phallic *double entendre*. Without this knowledge, it is nothing but a stylistic solecism. Comparing therefore the Munich version and the Moroder version is not simply a matter of counting what is included and what is left out, but of evaluating the degree of complexity that each version retains from Lang's overall scheme of alternation and parallel actions, his deployment of point-of-view editing, and his habit of forcing the viewer into retrospective revisions, by revealing a scene to have been less a direct representation of an action than accessed through someone's vision or fantasy.

Another example would be the scene in the Eternal Gardens: in Moroder's version, this starts with a tracking shot across the ensemble, the ladies of the night, the fountain of eternal youth, and the flora and fauna of Nirvana, before it cuts into the archly erotic chase. In Patalas's version, on the other hand, we cut from the stadium straight into the frolicking scene. Moroder's 'establishing shot' comes right at the end, and is in fact preceded by a glance-object shot of Freder, so that it now appears as the final survey of a world he is about to leave behind forever, struck as he has just been by an apparition that is to utterly transform his life. The shot mingles regret with disgust, leave-taking with leaving behind, as Freder dashes after the departing Maria. Similarly complex, in the Munich version, is the exchange of two kisses between Freder and Maria in the catacombs, each connoting a different stage of their relationship, each signifying an aspect of their strange spiritual journey of Caritas and Agape to Eros. Moroder, on the other hand, has opted for a single kiss, making their attraction for each other unambiguously erotic, if not overtly sexual. The extraordinary chasteness of the scene emphasised by Roland Schacht as a vital element of the plot (because it contrasts with the frankly pornographic allure of the false Maria) is thus lost in Moroder's version. Moroder's concern for the fire beneath Maria's demure attire, however, does prepare the audience more effectively for Rotwang's brutal and lustful visual rape that follows, as he tracks Maria with his flashlight, having obviously been a roused voyeur of the lovers' kiss.

Back to the Lab: The Murnau Stiftung Version

Since 1998, another archivist has been charged with assembling a new version of *Metropolis*. With funds from the Bundesarchiv (the post-unification Federal German Archive) – and moral support from Enno Patalas – but formally appointed by the rights holders, the Murnau Stiftung, in order to bring their own material up to the latest standard of film restoration, Martin Koerber has been sifting through all the available documentation and scholarship, as well as viewing scores of different prints. If he has not discovered new film material, he has none the less unearthed new film facts. In 1988, for instance, during a move of their film bunker from Neuß to Wiesbaden, the Murnau Stiftung discovered that it possessed a reel of the original intertitles, along with other nitrate material.[62] Unfortunately, after rescuing the intertitles they seem to have thrown most of the other cans away. Koerber's research represents the most up-to-date archival report, but he estimates that his version will not be completed before 2001, when it is to have its 'premiere' at the Berlin Film Festival. While he can draw on photographically much better material than any of the previous restorations – preferring, for instance, the Paramount negative to the MoMA print that served both the Munich version and Moroder as photographic base material – he too will not be able to present the 'original' *Metropolis* of the Berlin premiere:

> the scenes removed in 1927 by Paramount and then by UFA have not been found, and considering the many decades of intensive efforts around this film by the world's archives, it seems rather improbable that they are still hiding somewhere. This means that a quarter of the film, containing the core of the story as conceived by von Harbou and Lang must be considered lost forever.[63]

'The core of the story' of *Metropolis*? It seems that not only has the film mutated, so has our estimation of what its story is finally 'about'. For just as intriguing as the search for an *Ur-text* and an *Ur-copy* has become the question: what did these cuts and re-edits think they were doing, what story did they make the film tell, and how did history and time change this story, or rather, change our idea of the meaning of this film?

4
. . . .
INTERPRETING 'METROPOLIS': READING FOR THE PLOT

One definition of a classic is that it is a work which receives, or rather, provokes ever new interpretation. By this definition, *Metropolis* amply qualifies: whether because of the over-explicit moral, the inconsistencies of the plot, or the lacunary form by which the film has survived, each generation has proposed a reading, and in each case it has been as much a barometer of a period's own preferences and ideological preoccupations as a statement about the film.

The Social Question and Technology
In the 20s, uppermost in critics' minds was the so-called 'social question': did the film have anything to say about industrialisation as a factor preventing social unrest, or was it merely aggravating the class-struggle? Would modern technology enslave mankind or bring progress and prosperity to all? Overwhelmingly, the answer was that *Metropolis* had nothing to say on either, being far too cautious to show its hand other than by vapid symbolism and a pious motto.[64] The German communists were stridently scathing:

> This film, born out of bourgeois-capitalist ideology and produced with the insistently obtrusive intent to propagate the idea of class-reconciliation, the better to further capitalist methods of exploitation, only succeeds in unmasking the bourgeois worker-friendly phraseology in all its mendacity: this film is financed with the same capital that has pushed through the recent exploitative labour laws.[65]

The polemic clearly judges *Metropolis* in light of the industrial politics of the day, and according to some social historians, Weimar Germany's strategy regarding labour was divided, some industrialists tending towards the American model, where wages were allowed to rise in order to give the workers spending power. Looked at by sectors, the steel and coal industry in the mid-20s tended to be right-wing, while light manufacturing and branches of industry concerned with exports were generally more liberal. If one were to attach a party-political label, *Metropolis*'s 'solution' would reflect the moderate wing of the social democrats, even making room for trade union views. In fact, the offensive motto sounds remarkably like a trade union leader's address, assuring his members that 'Industry is holding its hand out to Labour.'[66]

Closely allied to the social question was the film's attitude to technology. Here, the technocrats as much as the political scientists felt let down: why did the cars look like yesterday's models; why were there fixed stairs and no escalators; why was automation resulting in exhausting and dangerous work for men rather than leading to monotonous, but light and safe tasks increasingly employing women? Where in Metropolis was the middle management, and where were the politicians, the police or security forces? To see workers exert huge physical effort manning a machine incensed every engineer, not only because it did not correspond to the facts of modern factory conditions, but because the very purpose of machines was to reduce industry's dependency on manual labour.[67] Several reviews explained why just about every piece of machinery shown in the film was non-functional, anachronistic and nonsensical even from the point of view of the rulers. The most vituperative comments came from H. G. Wells himself, in an article for the *New York Times* taking Lang and UFA to task for having made 'quite the silliest film' he had ever seen. He, too, itemised all the improbable, impossible and unexplained features of the world depicted in *Metropolis*, noting with special contempt the fact that Lang's city was organised top-down, when the city of the future would sprawl outwards into suburbs rather than stack its workers vertically.[68]

Generally, the dystopian vision of man's use of machines to aggravate exploitation and oppression rather than alleviate misery and want highly irritated social progressives, who saw the film give not only the wrong answer, but pose the wrong questions. Yet it also incensed the right-wing conservatives, because they understood the film as fuelling social tension, even advocating the class-struggle. Unresolved in this debate, and yet wholly underpinning it, was the relation of Weimar Germany to America. If *Metropolis* did not get to grips with the real effect of mechanisation and rationalisation, it was not least because Weimar Germany did not finally come to grips with Fordism and Taylorisation, just as the film industry never resolved its schizophrenic attitude to Hollywood.

Capitalist, Bolshevik or Proto-fascist?

It is here that Nazi film history tried to cut the Gordian knot. One of the few critical discussions of *Metropolis* during the Hitler era occurs in the UFA 25th anniversary volume, Otto Kriegk's 'The German Cinema in the Mirror of Ufa' (1943). The 'mirror' held up to *Metropolis* has a distinctly 'Alice through the Looking-Glass' logic. Kriegk attempts to resolve Nazi Germany's rivalry with the US mostly by deriding the folly of UFA even trying, and he projects onto the Soviet Union the Nazis' own military and expansionist ambitions:

> 'What an appalling film' shouted the critics, who until then had supported every cinematic work as long as it tried to out-do the Americans. Hundreds of cinephile intellectuals were deeply shocked when they realised to what heights of folly the attempt to have a world success at all cost could lead. With *Metropolis* the alien elements in the German cinema had reached the point of catastrophe. On the one hand, [the film] tried to imitate the soulless civilisation of America by going one better. Megalomania was matched with megalomania. If skyscraper was piled on skyscraper, surely those of New York would feel defeated [...]. Furthermore, if one added, the makers must have thought, enough of 'German spirituality' which was supposed to be superior to the American [way of life], and if one tackled the social question even more radically than the Americans were said to do, then one could not but pass the finishing line way ahead of them. [...]
>
> In Italy and Turkey the film was banned after a few showings. The reason given was the film's 'Bolshevik tendency'. In Germany at the time people of all political colours were baffled as to what could possibly be Bolshevik about the film. Today we know better. When the film opened in 1927, the Soviet Union was just preparing the phase of its technical revolution which we can now recognise as the precondition for the giant rearmament effort into which [Stalin ...] pressed the soulless masses, in order to [satisfy his] wild political ambitions.

Happily we are now immune to the dangers of such a nonsensical confusion of social problems. Nobody today would dream of throwing in one pot Marxism, dictatorship of the employers, superficial philanthropy and half-baked ideas about the decline of the West, give it the date-mark 2000, and then stir this pot so vigorously that the engagement of the son of a captain of industry to a girl of the people, playing Christ, could solve our social conflicts for the next thousand years.[69]

Disowning the film, Kriegk thus spares neither von Harbou's script nor the 'alien' (i.e. Jewish) input of Lang and Pommer. In fact, he makes the latter responsible for the commercial priorities the film industry set itself: '[UFA] wanted to produce whatever its export department considered good for sales, but in the end it achieved almost nothing abroad and very little in Germany.' Kriegk thus manages to turn the tables on the film's admirers as well as its detractors, calling it a Bolshevik film, made by Jewish liberals trying to ingratiate themselves with the Americans.

Only four years after Kriegk's put-down, one of the most damning (and influential) critiques that *Metropolis* was ever to receive was published in the US: Siegfried Kracauer's polemic attack on the film as proto-Nazi. In *From Caligari to Hitler* (1947) Kracauer also put *Metropolis* firmly in the dock; rather than being trivial or timid, or Bolshevik and aping Hollywood, Lang's film now put forward a right-wing utopia, giving the Weimar body-politic the shape of a social-fascist allegory. Furthermore, in its crowd-scenes, its spectacles of violence and destruction, it had like no other Weimar film inspired the Nazi aesthetic of the 'mass-ornament', implemented in Leni Riefenstahl's *Triumph of the Will*. For Kracauer, *Metropolis*'s 'message' could have been endorsed by Goebbels, the 'heart' now standing for propaganda, able to emotionally manipulate the working class. Especially reprehensible for Kracauer was the visual depiction of crowds. Pleasurable to the eye but politically totalitarian, Lang's geometrical forms in *Metropolis* deprive the masses of a will and reduce their public participation to a demagogic reflex. Rather than invoking the theatre work of Max Reinhardt and Erwin Piscator, as Lotte Eisner had done in *The Haunted Screen* (1969), Kracauer regarded Lang as the inventor of a new order of politicised spectacle, dangerous precisely because, fused into a crowd, individuals were encouraged to identify with a sense of community based not on intersubjective exchange or common interest, but on an all-seeing gaze, which they both identify with and submit to. Depicting the community in terms of vision and display, Lang's mass-ornament shapes a powerfully social space, contaminated by a new kind of (media-made) subjectivity, cut loose from political action and personal relations. It enacts this fascination of 'seeing oneself seen', however much the plot might critically decry such crowd formation:

> [I]n *Metropolis*, the decorative not only appears as an end in itself, but even belies certain points made by the plot. It makes sense that, on their way to and from the machines, the workers form ornamental groups; but it is nonsensical to force them into such groups while they are listening to a comforting speech from the girl Maria during their leisure time. In his exclusive concern with ornamentation Lang goes so far as to compose decorative patterns from the masses who are desperately trying to escape the inundation of the lower city. Cinematically an incomparable achievement, this inundation sequence is humanly a shocking failure.[70]

Thus both Kriegk and Kracauer condemn the film, for diametrically opposite reasons. Each regards it as a 'bad object' and assigns it a place in the ideological camp of the other. Notwithstanding Kracauer's infinitely more sophisticated and less self-contradictory reading, there are problems with his reading, too, especially when one considers that in the political context of 1924–8, UFA's commercial instincts would hardly have persuaded it to make a pro(to)-fascist film: the National Socialists only polled 2.6 per cent of the vote as late as the 1928 elections. As to the paternalist parable of class-collaboration which *Metropolis* is said to promote, it is explicitly ridiculed by Kriegk, who sees it as a typical fiction of (Jewish) bourgeois liberalism, not at all part of the Nazi creed. Instead of the Führer-principle so central to Nazi ideology, does not *Metropolis* show its Führer going down on his knees, fearing for his son? And what about the foreman, torn between loyalty to his place of work and the workers he represents, conscious of his bargaining power and only reluctantly agreeing to sue for industrial peace? Kracauer argued that this is precisely what makes the film so insidious. By seeming to give in to his son, Joh Fredersen actually tightens his hold over both the son (the

Weimar rebellion of the sons defeated by the Fathers) and the workers (because the appeals to their emotions make them blind to their own class-interests). But at the premiere of the restored version in Moscow, at the time of *perestroika*, a member of the audience came up to Enno Patalas and said: 'how topical the message of the film: this kind of reconciliation is exactly what we need.' Patalas wondered whether it was a communist film after all, or a sign of Russia's social-fascist ideology under Boris Yeltsin.[71] In the end, however, it was Kracauer's verdict of *Metropolis* as 'humanly a shocking failure' that has echoed down the decades, retrospectively giving the US public a moral bonus for not having fallen for the film at the box-office. Its failure, supposedly sealing the fate of UFA, which came under the control of Alfred Hugenberg, also seems just punishment for German hubris politically. The film's anti-humanist vision and anti-democratic perspective was made to serve as emblem for the tragic inadequacies of the Weimar Republic in the face of imminent fascism.

From 'Metropolis' to Mauthausen
Kracauer, of course, was not reading for the plot or the export intentions of UFA. It was the hidden tendencies, the political unconscious – the *monologue interieur* as he called it – of Weimar cinema that he tried to interpret, deliberately taking advantage of his hindsight position. After 1945 and in light of the terrible devastation that a top-down, regimented social system had brought to Europe, orchestrated by military high-technology and an efficient media machine that included the cinema, *Metropolis*'s planned nightmare city-state looked different from what it had before the war. Little did it matter that Nazism detested modernist architecture,[72] and that it promoted an anti-urban, 'blood-and-soil', back-to-the-land settlement policy. The film's complacently dystopic view of industrialisation, coupled with its evident fascination for the terrible beauty of outsize machines as well as Lang's penchant for disasters and *Götterdämmerung* came back to haunt the director. *Metropolis* now seemed to prove that Lang never did make up his mind between baleful prediction and self-fulfilling prophecy, the childish plot discrediting the warning message, while the childlike pleasure in the magic of electricity endorsed a dangerous play with fire:

> The superbly realised sequence in which the evil scientist creates his robot has a bizarre quality which the current science fiction films have

never equalled, but it is legitimate to ask how important in the film's context – it has, after all, a very serious theme – it is to show all the glamorous electronic devices and to let the audience marvel at the big sparks, while the main issues are being fought out between capital and labour. This child-like insistence on Lang's part in having fun with huge scientific gadgets remains the film's main source of appeal.[73]

Whatever ambiguity had been felt in the 20s about *Metropolis*, Kracauer's interpretation from 1947 carried the day. It was as if his reading allowed one to re-live, indeed to participate in the very birth of Nazi ideology and its aesthetic in an apparently most unsuspected guise. But was the film unwittingly prophetic, anticipatory or actively collusive? This question was also raised by another feature of *Metropolis* that only hindsight had allowed to appear.

One of the most impressive visions in the film is that of Moloch, the man-devouring machine. Woven into the narrative via the *Book of Revelations* which Freder has by his bedside table,[74] its metaphoric meaning is that of a machine exacting human sacrifices. But a look at von Harbou's novel also suggests a further reading, for there, one of the main themes is that of 'food' or 'fodder'. Both in the opening scene of the shift change and in Freder's Moloch vision, von Harbou develops the image of the city's machines needing 'living fodder, the endless stream of human beings processed through the machine rooms, all those men used up, and spat out at the other end'.[75] Later on, it is the false Maria who tells the workers: 'you are just fodder for machines.' One can interpret this motif psychoanalytically, seeing it as part of the oral–anal sadistic fantasy underpinning the Oedipal scenario that the film elaborates around Freder's castration anxiety, but it could also explain why these workers do not produce anything useful, a feature that so puzzled Anglo-American critics. What if the machines of Metropolis did not refer to industrial production in the conventional sense at all? In the way they ingest, devour, and then excrete human beings, they take up instead the metaphor of the total war machine, which so powerfully obsessed literature and the arts after the First World War. There, Moloch was the God of War, a machine destroying machines and devouring soldiers as 'cannon-fodder'. Yet after the Second World War, such an imagery of human beings used up as brute matter would inevitably associate neither the First nor the Second World War, but another 'by-product' of Nazirule, the Holocaust and the death camps. Metropolis's anticipatory scenario would thus be of a society that works people to death, even when the work is socially unproductive. The film historian Georges Sadoul, writing in the mid-60s picked up this association, quoting a man arriving at the Mauthausen concentration camp in 1943. As he ascends the ramp, seeing all these men and women in uniform and shaven heads, he is heard saying to his fellow-prisoner: 'connais-tu *Metropolis*?'[76]

'Metropolis' in 'Gravity's Rainbow'

This train of associations turns up, more indirectly and obliquely, in Thomas Pynchon's novel. An often overlooked but oddly telling source for charting the change in the fortunes of *Metropolis* as a classic text of dystopic modernity into a cult classic of several kinds of cynically enlightened postmodernities, Pynchon at once follows in Kracauer's footsteps, but also pre-dates Moroder's re-charging of the film's various energy levels. *Gravity's Rainbow* places its references to *Metropolis* at a very precise moment in European history, namely 1945, when the technological advances inaugurating the space age of moon rockets, jet-engines and smart bombs still show traces of the Allied Powers' political compromise with fascism. In this Second World War epic, one of the main protagonists is Franz Pökler, an ominously eloquent and yet symptomatic fan of Fritz Lang's German films, and especially *Metropolis*. A scientist who during the last years of the Nazi regime worked on Hitler's secret

weapon, the V2 rocket system at both Peenemünde and the notorious 'Dora' camp in Nordhausen, Pökler recalls the Weimar years 'through inflation and depression'. His *Zeitgeist* 'came to have a human face attached to it, *natürlich* that of the actor Rudolf Klein-Rogge whom Pökler idolised and wanted to be like'. Debriefed by the Americans about the brain behind the V2 rocket,

The human face of the Weimar years: Rudolf Klein-Rogge (Stiftung Deutsche Kinemathek Berlin)

supposedly a former Professor at the Munich Technische Hochschule in the 20s, Pökler confuses him with Rotwang and he muses about *Metropolis*:

> Great movie. Exactly the world Pökler and evidently quite a few others were dreaming about in those days, a corporate City-State where technology was the source of power, the engineer worked closely with the administrator, the masses laboured unseen far underground, and ultimate power lay with a single leader at the top, fatherly and benevolent and just, who wore magnificent-looking suits and whose name Pökler couldn't remember, being too taken with Klein-Rogge playing the mad inventor, [... a man] indispensable to those who ran the metropolis, yet at the end the untameable lion who could let it all crash, girl, State, masses, himself, asserting his reality against them all in one last roaring plunge from rooftop to street.[77]

This colourful passage confirms Kracauer's intuition that Lang's film allowed viewers to nourish some very potent fantasies of absolute power and self-destruction, but Pynchon extends it to include the role Nazi scientists like Wernher von Braun were to play in winning the Space Race for the US, forcibly reminding the reader of the price such science had extracted from the human beings working in forced labour camps and Hitler's death-mills.

Pökler is a useful witness, since he is obviously sympathetic to the film ideologically, yet his emotions are invested not in the class-collaborationist parable, but rather in the disjuncture between a technocratic elite and the masses it is supposed to serve, but actually despises. A second film within the film, one responding to another kind of temperature, so to speak, seems to have carried away the first, the narrative one of the conciliatory, redemptive ending, and instead concluding with the 'untameable lion's death. Read from the point of view of Rotwang, *Metropolis* appears most truthful where it insists on the persistence of the archaic-anarchic aspects, but also the mythic dimension of the technological-rationalist fantasy that social progressives like H. G. Wells found so anachronistic and deplorable. Pökler's evident disregard for the plot's numerous twists and turns is thus interesting in light of the howls of protest that greeted the film originally, when its ideological naïveties and narrative incoherence were almost universally ridiculed.

In this sense, Pynchon's Pökler is a link between Kracauer's interpretation and another of Kracauer's apparent diametrical opposites, the postmodern, pop-rock or cyber-punk revaluation of *Metropolis* as a cult classic of Generation X. Pynchon's *Metropolis* is, after all, also about terrific suits and style-wars as much as it is about the imaginary self-image of the 'a-political' military-industrial complex entering into a direct alliance with the political establishment, if necessary proto-fascist, so long as it upheld the knowledge-based state-within-the-state of special interest lobbies, military quangos, and above-the-law secret services. Pynchon's vision, however, is also the beginning of the urbanist fantasies that the 80s were to spin so persuasively around *Metropolis*, and he indirectly confirms that Lang was one of the first directors to envisage an ideological role for cinema's impact not on politics, but on designer-politics. *Metropolis* did in this sense pioneer one of the effects that blockbuster film-making has had on related consumer industries (clothes, fabrics, furnishings, personal accessories), as well as on modern politics, whether democratic or totalitarian, utilising an eclectic modernism of spectacle and seriality. The mass-ornament so abhorred by Kracauer as undemocratic and totalitarian would in due course become a key element of consumerist capitalism, where there is no object, gesture or expression that is not styled, 'designed', aware that it is being looked at. It is as if Lang had sensed that a debate which merely contrasted machines as either instruments of enslavement or as mankind's liberators was already obsolete by 1927. 'I want to be a machine' is a saying attributed to Andy Warhol. It could have been the alternative motto of *Metropolis*, making Lang's supposed anti-humanism look more like an anticipated post-humanism.

Fairy-tales, Machines and Oedipus

Perhaps one reason why Lang's film weathered so well the contradictory treatment it received across the decades is that it has the robustness of a fairy-tale. Such stories survive rough handling thanks to their redundancies and archetypal configurations. UFA rivalled US films not only in size and special effects, it also wanted to present a romance for the machine age, a story as previously only the Americans had known how to tell. Although not fulfilling UFA's hopes, *Metropolis* rather accurately reproduced the double plot structure of Hollywood classical narrative, interweaving fairy-tale and romance with an adventure plot and quest. Already Roland Schacht had noticed the effect obtained: the story, he argued, deposits its schematic opposition between workers and bosses inside a *Märchen*, a fairy-tale, which it complicates by two additional intrigues. Besides the romance of Freder and Maria, there is the romantic-Gothic fairy-tale of the sorcerer's apprentice: an inventor creates an artificial human being that brings disaster to all concerned. Set against this is the intrigue centred on 'Slim' – the eyes and ears of Metropolis's master – and his ultimately foiled attempts to neutralise the hero's helpers. The second intrigue is Rotwang's revenge, trying to destroy the son of the man who took away his love. Schacht saw the long shadow of *The Hunchback of Notre Dame* (one of whose many filmed versions was shown in Berlin in 1925) falling on the tale, alluded to in the gargoyle-guarded Cathedral parapet which is the site for the final showdown. Rotwang as the hunchback Quasimodo as well as a demonic Dr Frankenstein brings forth further parallels: in each case, a blond but bland youthful hero contends for a fair maiden whose alter ego is an evil witch. A historical novel, heavily influenced by Walter Scott, *Notre Dame de Paris* – like *Metropolis* – mixes redemptive religion and a messiah-figure, supported by a virginal female, with an easily stirred rabble-crowd in a heady brew of post-Revolutionary anxieties. Given this stab at Hollywood-style story construction, it seems particularly ironic that in the US release version both of the adventure plots fell victim to Paramount's savage cuts, thus seriously unbalancing the narrative

Rotwang's bachelor machine: malevolent robot or empowering cyborg?

design. On the other hand, the thought that *Metropolis* might have been inspired by Walter Scott and Victor Hugo as much as it was beholden to H. G. Wells and Villiers de l'Isle-Adam is intriguing. It is picked up indirectly in the 70s, after the structuralist turn, when Vladimir Propp, Claude Levi-Strauss and Greimas provided the theoretical models for analysing popular narratives such as this.

Focusing on the fairy-tale and quest elements in *Metropolis*, Alan Williams and John Tulloch's essays present structuralist versions of the Oedipal conflict, endorsing Kracauer's thesis of 'the adolescent and the whore', (i.e. the split maternal figure), but refraining from drawing Kracauer's more explicit political conclusions. For the structuralists, Lang/von Harbou's mythopoetic scheme fits into a broader ideological model of popular story-telling as the imaginary resolution to real contradictions, and they see the film respond to Weimar's political deadlocks, while addressing anxieties over masculinity and authority. Tulloch, following Lucien Goldman's genetic structuralism, discovers a dialectical movement propelling the film, where the thesis is expressed in Maria's first words: 'all men are brothers.' The antithesis would be that in practice, brain and hands are separated. The synthesis – the establishment of true brotherhood – requires the intervention not so much of Freder as mediator, but of the female element, itself purged of its own excesses (the sexualised robot) and acting through the male (Maria steering Freder): a benignly matriarchal rewriting of both the Sleeping Beauty story and the Christian myth of Mary and Jesus. Williams' Greimasian approach brings out the basic contradiction as a constitutive 'lack', located in the workers' absence of control over their existence. The task of the narrative is to move that which embodies the lack from one space to another, effectively making the worker's children the object of transfer and exchange. Parallel to this story is that of Freder, also driven by lack: not knowing how miserable the workers' lives are. For him, knowledge becomes the object, and it, too requires a transfer across different spaces: machine room, Fredersen's office, the catacombs. Williams' analysis highlights the mirroring function of certain scenes, such as the eternal gardens and the catacombs. He also underscores the central importance of Maria, since she participates in several different transactions: so many in fact, that she has to be split in two, in order to fulfil all the symbolic tasks required, including that of being the lack-embodying object for Rotwang and Freder. Her role involves such archetypal fairy-tale moves as kidnap, foiled rescue, the hero's fight with the sorcerer and eventual release of the 'princess' and restitution to her rightful place.

Apart from the folk-tale elements, neither the Virgin Mary symbolism nor the split between virgin and whore had escaped earlier commentators, but in the cynical Berlin atmosphere of 1927, the figure of Maria was greeted with undisguised derision. Like the taste-based division of labour between Lang and von Harbou, it was a gender discourse that all too plainly spoke a male-chauvinist language. Lang's brilliant film technique had male attributes of control and mastery, while comments on the 'kitsch' characters, and especially Maria, came with unflattering female connotations, such as 'Kurfürstendämchen' (a pun on Berlin's fashionable shopping area and the diminutive for 'lady'), 'violet-hued Biedermeier', 'ladies' home journal romanticism'. Yet why, other than to provide the plot with extra symmetries, did Rotwang fashion a robot with female features? This was a question that had apparently not struck many critics until the mid-70s. Whether it was the result of feminist film theory, or the discovery of von Harbou's script of *Metropolis*, the robot Maria and the role played by the excised Hel suddenly came into the spotlight. By the late-70s and early 80s questions of patriarchy and male paranoia, rephrased in terms of gender theory, had occupied centre-stage. Traditionally, *Metropolis* had been seen as a love story between Freder and Maria, with all the complications and delays of classical Hollywood plotting, where Freder can only win 'the girl' by defeating the Father, which he does by first taking the side of the workers in their struggle, and then, by engaging in a proxy fight with the 'bad' father, Rotwang, over the possession of the Mother. Yet the references to Hel, now that they have been put back, make the real Maria the symbolic double of Freder's mother, as well as Rotwang's lost love and Fredersen's wife. The false Maria is the 'other woman', *femme fatale*, whore and rabble-rouser. Centred on the absent mother, and thereby multiplying the father–son relationships, the intrigue transforms the woman into an object of desire without having to acknowledge her sexuality, a strategy typical of narratives constructed around male narcissism. For Rotwang, Maria is a substitute of the dead Hel, symbolised in the robot, itself a phallic representation of Rotwang's missing hand; for Freder, she is the mother he never knew; and, for his father, the woman that can be controlled and manipulated wholly as image. In other words, *Metropolis*'s darker fantasies could be psychoanalytically decoded: Freder's castration anxiety and the fetishised image of woman did indeed receive ample textual, as well as contextual attention.[78] In his influential essay 'The Vamp and the Machine', Andreas Huyssen took up two traditional Weimar motifs, the anxious male and the intellectuals' technophobic cultural pessimism. His central thesis was that the film manages an ingeniously original 'resolution' to these two complexes by constructing a fable in which the (culturally recent) fear of 'technology out of control' is mapped onto the (more archaic) fear of 'female sexuality out of control'. The move at the ideological level has its stylistic correspondence: the characters' language of Expressionist pathos is eventually contained by the *Neue Sachlichkeit* cool of the machine aesthetics.[79]

Huyssen saw the robot's female gender as a conservative counter-strategy: through the false Maria, *Metropolis* demonises female sexuality, and her threat justifies the male fantasy of strong leadership, needed to keep the forces of the feminised masses as well as of a potentially destructive technology under firm control. In a society where paternal authority had been undermined by the lost war and the humiliating conditions of the subsequent peace, such a scenario was anti-socialist and anti-feminist, but served deep-seated collective psychic needs. This is Kracauer updated, backed by an impressive historical survey of the gendering of technology in German art and literature from the mid-nineteenth century onwards. It explains why Freder is weak, ineffectual, never quite at the right place at the right time, and why, despite charging impulsively with his head thrust forward, he frequently clutches at his heart or backs off in horror at what he sees. Huyssen's argument, on the other hand, downplays the Oedipal drama around Freder, who – via the robot Maria – realises that he has two father figures, as well as two maternal imagos, the saintly and the sexualised one. His personal quest unfolds in the direction of having to rid himself of both Rotwang and the robot, symbolising the disruptive doubles troubling his male identity. Only once this task is accomplished can he function as mediator, effectively having taken over from his father the role of the adult male, subject to his society's symbolic order. In the course of this, Freder has to bring his inhuman, de-sexualised father back into the community of feeling, which happens when Fredersen begins to show anxiety for his

Freder, stunned by the man-
eating Moloch

son, down on the Cathedral steps, rather than continuing to shut himself up in his grief for Hel, high above the city. He, too, like Rotwang is motivated by the absent Hel, whose loss he represses by asking the wizard to create a woman, outwardly enticing like a *femme fatale*, but inwardly calculating like a man. Another reading of this plot point is offered by Anton Kaes:

> Who, then, is left out of [the] harmonious ending? It is Rotwang [...], dressed like an Eastern Jew or like Rabbi Loew in Paul Wegener's 1920s *The Golem* [... and] the female robot, who is burnt at the stake. Eliminating the double threat of a 'scheming Jewish scientist' and the new woman as femme fatale (both marked as menacing outsiders) means, within the narrative logic of the film, eliminating the archetypes of cold rationality and uncontrollable sexuality, both seen as mortal dangers to the spirit of the community. What remains is a transformed community that again embraces technology that is now free, the film insinuates, from 'Jewish control' and infused instead with German spirituality.[80]

Kaes's terms echo those of Kriegk, but once again, with a kind of figure/ground reversal as to the film's ideological meaning, proving Kaes's other point, namely that a 'dialectic of modernity' runs through almost all cultural manifestations of Weimar Germany, making attributions of political bias slippery. What remains remarkable about *Metropolis* is once again its power to compress this dialectic – made up of so many contradictory motifs and themes – into one story-line.

5

....

'METROPOLIS', MORODER AND SOUND

If the logic of these successive critical moves is followed through, it comes as something of a surprise to realise that a quite different reading of *Metropolis* has emerged since the mid-80s. Resolutely turning away from anxious males, man-eating machines and *femmes fatales*, from the masses, fascism and the class-struggle, the 80s and 90s have made the city itself the main protagonist: the mega-city not so much of the future, but the vanishing point of all contemporary urbanist fantasies of entertainment spaces and spectacle environments. These mega-cities in turn have spawned their own mutant bodies, so that the undisputed star of the film has become the robot, no longer called by that name, but morphed into the 'replicant' and 'cyborg': the metal-sheathed Madonna-virgin in Rotwang's lab is now a post-human, post-gender figure of ambiguous, but ultimately positive appeal, prototype of the female rock star and the pop-performer. The reversal suggests that by the turn of the century we have ceased to fear technology as invasive, so deeply has it penetrated into the spheres of subjectivity and sexuality. Instead, men and women seem happy to acquire as prosthetic extensions of their selves all manner of technical devices, domesticated in the culture of the 'personal' gadget and exoticised in the mode of performative display.

The most persuasive manifestations of this new take on technology and subjectivity are on the whole found in the cinema itself: the many references to icons, images or scenes from *Metropolis* in such 'modern classics' as *Batman Returns* (1992) and *Star Wars* (1977), *Brazil* (1985), *Terminator II* (1991), *Se7en* (1995), *Dark City* (1998) and *The Fifth Element* (1997). Above all Ridley Scott's *Blade Runner* (1982) presents a remarkably faithful and yet topically transformed reprise of the basic story of *Metropolis*,[81] making it the inevitable precursor of a post-60s, but also post-Fordist and post-colonial, vision of the mega-city as corporate state, driven by the globalising forces of migrant labour, mass entertainment and cult religion.

Performance Pieces and Sound Spaces: Seeing Lang with Moroder's Ears
Such a turn of events positions Moroder's version of *Metropolis* at a pivotal point, no longer merely between archival restoration and

postmodern pastiche. Rather, it partakes in a broader cultural shift, away from 'reconstruction' and 'interpretation' altogether and closer to the gesture of sampling, selective appropriation and even cannibalising incorporation. The desire to 'perform' *Metropolis*, instead of putting it in a critical or historical perspective, is largely responsible for lending new life to the vision of Lang and von Harbou. The key element is probably the changing place of music and sound not only in this film, but in popular visual culture generally. Moroder's intuition was to make the matinee 'silents' seen on television big again – big screen, big sound, big budget. Not driven to revive the phantom 'first night' of archivists and historians, he treated the film (at once respectfully and provocatively) as a *found object*. In so doing, his archival digging, his money and technical effort restored not the print, but what could be called *Metropolis*'s 'innocence', simulating an illusion of pristine presence that made this 'fallen woman' of a film once more 'like a virgin'.

To some, such treatment and especially the New Wave music track compounded heresy with blasphemy, adding a special cynicism to iconoclast insouciance. But it was also a bold move, for it took for granted that since the 70s, a film experience is above all also a sound experience, and a sound experience is always also an experience of space. Moroder the composer took the peremptory, but intricate forms of synchronisation between sound-source and image-track that have become the norm since the introduction of Dolby stereo as the basis of his meticulous and competent workmanship. If the model was indeed the music video, much of whose artistry goes into devising new sound-image bridges – with the sound often cueing the image, rather than vice versa, as in classical sound cinema – then the implications were broader than the obligatory mention of MTV suggests. He turned *Metropolis* above all into a space to inhabit, rather than a story to follow or an ideology to work through and demystify. Contrary to the rules of classical continuity editing, which often allocate to sound the role of effacing itself in the service of the image, Dolby sound and disco beat are anything but self-effacing. In the case of *Metropolis*, Lang's idiosyncratic visual style, with its sudden changes of angle, the startling montage-effects, the dramatic shifts in size, and the Expressionist play on shape and line – which in the 'silent version' often feels like irritating ornament and a distraction from the narrative – becomes, thanks to Moroder, not only visible to the trained eye, but palpable as an immediate, bodily experience. A full instrumental score without the songs – the latter necessary for the commercial surplus value of tape and CD sales – might have been better, giving Moroder's synthesiser sound space even more scope to penetrate, model and modulate the visual space of Lang's film, vibrating as it now does with an inner movement of shape, depth and texture. Moroder was evidently aware of this, for he prefaced the film with a quotation from Lang: 'I perceive the world through the eye and only very rarely through the ear, much to my regret.'

Moroder's score, perhaps by its deliberate anachronisms, induces one to discover Lang's images afresh: projected not on a two-dimensional screen but into the stereophonic space created by the sounds, though without making *Metropolis* thereby more 'hyper-real' (as digital special effects tend to do). On the contrary, the element of abstraction, the tension between the functional and the ornamental in Lang's *mise en scène* of places, objects and people (for which, as we saw, he was duly taken to task by Kracauer) once more conveys the vitality that modernism's constructivist forms possessed for artists like Léger or Malevich, at a time when Taylorisation and biomechanics appealed to both V. I. Lenin and Henry Ford. Two years after *Metropolis*, in 1929, Erich Kettelhut summarised his first experience with film sound:

> Speech, song, music and sound-effects must affect the spectator in the auditorium not as sounds emanating from somewhere in the auditorium or from behind the screen, but directly from the screen image. It is the film image itself which must become even more optical, plastic, closer to reality and even more authentic if the sound is to reproduce as living [...]. Should we be in a position to create a three-dimensional film image, then the sound will be there to provide the extra dimension.[82]

Whatever pained expressions cross one's face when confronted with lyrics like 'Here She Comes', 'Cage of Freedom' or (disarmingly candid) 'What's Going On?', Moroder's sound thus serves Lang curiously well.[83] Especially in the set-pieces (the cityscape, the machine room, the transformation of Maria, the flooding of the workers' homes) the new sound effects for *Metropolis* provide a breathtaking and awesome sense of spectacle that puts to shame much of the special effect work one has come to associate with contemporary Hollywood. The thrills, of course, have

The workers' quarters flooded

At the Tower of Babel: shaven slaves poised for mayhem

less to do with the suitability of the score as theme music for this particular narrative. Refusing to interpret the story or the characters except in the most banal way, the music instead inhabits the screen image, enhancing one's perception of other dimensions. The toning in different shades of pink (rather than sepia) and ice-blue (rather than cobalt) gives the black-and-white the high artifice of colour while preserving the richness of tonal values one associates with mint-condition silent prints, although the luminous brilliance, so seductive to the eye, is no doubt a synaesthetic illusion due to the metallic crispness of the Dolby score.

The film is in the service of tactile as much as specular delights, further insinuating it into the *Zeitgeist* of the 80s. For although it may not be obvious what punk fashion, New Wave music and strobe-light stage acts have in common with the constructivist ethos of the 20s (except perhaps a pessimism that is both energetic and sentimental), the shaven heads of the Babylonian slaves, the workers' thick platform shoes, the leather-clad figures guarding the mouth of Moloch, or Klein-Rogge's inspired mad scientist Rotwang are instantly recognisable icons of the 80s, whatever they may have meant in and for the 20s. *Metropolis* Moroder-style makes it even more apparent that Fritz Lang was not only an architect, but also an *ensemblier* of genius. Eclectic and decorative, he could none the less design a consistent look, from dressing a huge set to arranging the tiniest accessories on a bedside table, while giving them enough variation to convey a quite particular visual rhythm. Even in static compositions he counterpoints a dominant visual motif by repeating it several times in echoing shapes, playing on differences of size and surface texture. The many three-way relations of the plot are taken up in the ziggurats and

The steam-whistle's screams of light

pyramid shapes of the high-rises, the patterned triangles of parquet floors and light fixtures, the rhomboid wedges of the pistons. They recur as arrows and chevrons in Rotwang's lab and the machine room, or as graphic geometry in the intertitles. Varied, inverted or serialised, they transform mere decorative elements into constructivist principles: wedges and circles, lines and cubes fight it out among each other, as in a Malevich painting. Many of these visual contests Moroder's version is able to pick out, correlating Lang's jaggedly dynamic compositions with his own syncopated sound and translating Lang's editing effects into rock harmonies, as in the opening scene when the music works with predictable precision towards the climax of the steam-whistle blowing to announce the end of the shift.

Appropriation in Place of Interpretation?

Moroder's formula, however, may not be repeatable (though the French did coin for such jazzed-up adaptations the verb *moroder*). There have been several attempts – including a stage musical[84] – to extend the experiment, and turn *Metropolis* into a kind of visual score, ready to be performed in very different musical idioms. Full orchestra and chamber music archive screenings – whether with the Munich print or another version – have become staple repertoire attractions, possibly also in order to claw back some of the prestige of a high-culture event for a film that first came back from the dead in Moroder's downmarket version.[85] The conductor Berndt Heller, known for spectacular stage shows of both classical music and light entertainment, regularly toured with the film in the 80s. A 1988 performance at the Munich Gasteig Philharmonie led a reviewer to observe that

> the many voices of the instruments made the plot not less but more transparent, uniting the disparate elements of the story. Paradoxically, the live musical accompaniment [also] tempered the often barely supportable pathos. [...] The full body [of the orchestra] placed in front of the screen created a new sound space, forming a sort of entrance lobby leading up to the images. In truth, the film should have been projected against the Gasteig facade. The walls would have sent back the images like an echo.[86]

After German unification Heller also gave a special 1992 Berlin Film Festival performance at Babelsberg, 'at the very site where [the film] was made'.[87]

Metropolis, as Patalas rightly perceived when he advised Moroder, was the inevitable choice for this kind of sound space as well as for these kinds of commercial instincts, not only because the film was itself the brainchild of brilliant entrepreneurial opportunism. It is that rare case of a 'silent' film where the addition of (live or Dolby) sound exposes a deeper truth about European cinema generally, forcing the abstracting, 'purist' and serialising tendencies of late 20s avant-garde cinema to confront the various new technologies of speech, sound and haptic vision, at the point where they transformed themselves into a culture of commodities, inviting touch and possession. But Lang also understood that cinema would exercise its power of fascination through exhibitionist spectacle as well as voyeuristic surveillance. In both respects, *Metropolis* has become 'more like itself' in the uncanny guise that Moroder gave it than it had ever been before. As a film that one now inhabits rather than interprets, it is as much an experience to dress up and be seen in, as it is a film to see and be addressed by. 'Innocence restored' I called Moroder's move above, possibly rather too flippantly.[88] Better perhaps to invoke Walter Benjamin's famous description of the 'true collector': someone 'to whom ownership is the most intimate relationship one can have to objects. Not that they come alive in him; it is he who lives in them.'[89] If one substitutes 'true fan' for 'true collector', one is as close as can be to the kind of 'heart' that in Moroder's case has mediated between *Metropolis* the film history classic and *Metropolis* the cult classic.

The City-machine: Urbanist Fantasies and Designer Nightmares

Dear Mr Lang, don't always think in terms of individual images! Your problem is that the idea counts as nothing for you, the only thing that matters is the image. [...] And, of course, many of your images are very beautiful, the technique is excellent, but shouldn't they also have meaning and sense?[90]

The exasperated reviewer was not far off the mark. Film critics of the realist persuasion have always preferred the horizontality of meaning and the linearity of sense to the verticality of montage and the 'diagonal symphonies' of abstraction. The miracle of *Metropolis* in this respect is how much of the vertical thinking of a Ruttmann, Viking Eggeling and Hans Richter Lang had been able to translate (*traductore/traditore?*) into a narrative feature film.[91] En passant, he also saluted Ferdinand Léger and Francis Picabia's *Ballet mécanique*, Jakov Protasanov's *Aelita* and Marcel L'Herbier's *L'Inhumaine* (all 1924). By the time he came to make *Metropolis*, the machine aesthetic had already migrated from the formal language of the avant-garde to the vocabulary of the cultural critic. As if anticipating both *Metropolis* and Ruttmann's *Berlin – Symphony of a Big City*, Egon Friedell, for instance, had described Berlin in 1912 as

> a wonderful modern engine-room, a giant electrical motor, which executes with incredible precision, speed and energy a plethora of complicated, mechanical tasks. True, so far the machine lacks a soul. The life of Berlin is the life of a cinematograph theatre, the life of a brilliantly constructed homunculus-machine.[92]

Conversely, as if commenting on Friedell's pre-war euphoria, *Metropolis* is not so much a film about machines as it is itself a machine, made up of parts fitted together, whose intricate clockwork elements are as much the human passions, anxieties and aggressions as they are the pistons, flywheels and dials. A specific example from *Metropolis* would be the scene where Freder has just discovered the workers underground. He is dismayed by the plight of the man at the big dial who with his two arms has to align three hands on a clock face so that they touch the intermittently flashing lights arranged in a circle. The man collapses and Freder rushes to take over in order to avert danger. But he is incapable of servicing the controls with sufficient dexterity and speed, so that he is forced to his knees half carrying the hands like Atlas supporting the Globe, half suspended from them like Christ at the cross. The image is so startling because it represents an impossible task: nothing seems to connect these hands to the overall mechanism of the machine and yet everything depends on the hands making contact with the lights in a particular sequence.[93]

The overlay in one image of inert arbitrariness (represented by the three limply hanging hands as Freder has to let go) and of implacable necessity (repeating a series of movements as if doing them forever) makes the scene at once comically surreal and deeply frightening, embodied in Freder's emotionally ambiguous posture. For after a few moments, another image superimposes itself over Freder at the dial: that of a spare elegant wall clock, its hour and minute hands rigidly in place, and only the slender third hand, ticking away as it mounts from mid-point to the full minute. The effect is the more shocking since it is this serene image of the wall clock that suggests an altogether different violence: its regular movement is irreversible and unstoppable. An invisible but functioning mechanism keeps the hands in place and in its self-sufficient art-deco beauty, the object ridicules Freder's Expressionist contortions of anguish and exhaustion. If man could disappear, or at least turn himself into a machine, the scene seems to say, there would be no need for conflict or struggle. The violence of the modern functional object as it presents its smooth surface and imperturbably regular motion to the eye all but disguises the extent to which the fading image is cancelled not just visually, but contradicted by the one that follows. The annihilation, however, is not in the image but resides in the transfer of meaning that the superimposition gives to the neutrality of the clock. Its hands seem to 'pick up' the inert ones of the dial, but instead of echoing Freder's effort, the clock distances itself from him by its indifference. Wheels within wheels, one is tempted to resume, moving inexorably towards entropy and exhaustion. But the scene just described is itself embedded in another shot: that of Joh Fredersen, waiting in Rotwang's office, idly looking at his wristwatch in expectation of the shift-change. Yet while all the official clocks of the metropolis have faces divided into ten units – the metric time of the machine – the close-up of Fredersen's time-piece shows Fritz Lang's own expensive Swiss watch, on which the day is evidently divided into twelve hours. In a typically ironic, self-referential gesture, the master of Metropolis and watchmaker of its universe declares himself both part of his world and standing apart from it.

Such is the studied ambiguity of Lang that in his film 'machines [signify] not as tools but as a life-style'.[94] What the more recent status of *Metropolis* as a cult classic – to be performed and to inhabit – therefore encourages is another look at the film's design and Weimar cinema architecture. If the sound spaces (whether Moroder's, Huppertz', Heller's or those of a Jazz trio) make Lang's film enter inevitably into the fun culture and fantasy environments of today, they also allow one to experience the sheer plasticity of Lang's vision as if for the first time. With Moroder, I suggested, *Metropolis* left behind party politics and even gender politics, in order to become the archetypal cinematic city film. As it became an art director's Aladdin's Cave to steal from or to strip-mine for images of urban anomie, it likewise nurtured euphoric fantasies of the city machine in the spirit of Le Corbusier, or latterly, Rem Koolhaas's *Delirious New York*. Here, too, Moroder may have spoken truer than he knew. For one does not have to probe this paradigm of the cinematic city too deeply before *Metropolis* reveals itself responding very precisely to the architectural and urbanist debates of the 20s. Insofar as these focused on the desirability of skyscrapers, embraced by modernist city planners, but rejected by communists, socialists and social reformers, *Metropolis* resumes yet another dialectic of modernity. Dietrich Neumann has shown how the different types of cityscape drawn by Hunte and Kettelhut freely borrowed from the designs of the top architects of the day who had been toying with 'revolutionary' projects since 1910, and whose enforced idleness during the First World War and in the immediate post-war years had made them work on all manner of daringly futuristic but never-to-be-realised designs.[95] Some of the 'idleness' came to an abrupt end with the 1921 competition for Berlin's first multi-purpose high-rise office block near the Friedrichstrasse's inner-city railway station. As 'Der Schrei nach dem Turmhaus' ('the cry for a tower-house') the forty-odd submissions have entered architectural history, mainly because of Mies van der Rohe's revolutionary design of a glass-fronted curtain-wall skyscraper, not even placed by the judges, but

hotly discussed in the press and professional journals for years to come.[96] Lang's undoubted awareness of this debate adds another layer of Weimar Germany's cultural history to the (con)founding myth of how the Manhattan skyline was supposed to have been the main source of inspiration.[97]

Metropolis was not only influenced by, but took a stand on the *Turmhaus* and *Stadtkrone* debates. It explains why Lang's city as well as his

Design from 'Der Schrei nach dem Turmhaus', Berlin Friedrichstrasse, 1921 story are organised in such a ruthlessly vertical way, which – as H. G. Wells scornfully but perhaps too hastily pointed out – flies in the face of all commensense and expert extrapolations. They predicted horizontal growth, mass transport and a suburban sprawl as the more likely solutions for the housing problems of the working class. Lang's up-down, paternoster division of architectural forms into a language of the class-struggle, however, does not argue the case for or against a particular type of building and its urbanist consequences. Rather, it exploits the potential of the vertical as a universally understood metaphor of social power, a pressure scale and measuring gauge, as well as drawing a historical time-line that reaches from the 'tomorrowland' of the penthouse suite to the 'times immemorial' of the catacombs. It also marks Fredersen's journey from omniscient hubris to the humility of the Cathedral steps, while the children progress from the Workers' City below to the Eternal Gardens above. The stark symbol of the New Tower of Babel skyscraper may have spurned Weimar Germany's urban pragmatists and socialist reformers, trying to devise the liveable city of the future. But its crown of thorns none the less supplied a memorable visual rhyme for a hero crucified on the dials of an underground infernal machine. However much he may have lagged 'behind' the planners, Lang was in the end also in front, when one considers how – first in the 30s with New York's Radio City project, and then from the 70s onwards all over the world – tall buildings have become the universally accepted architectural language of civic identities, tourist landmarks and corporate statements. That a different kind of life may well exist at street level or 'underground', at once vital and volatile, oppressed and messy, is an insight also preserved by the film, however muted the energy of the Worker's City may appear in its wedge-shaped formation at the end.[98]

CONCLUSION

Reviewing the six decades of reviews of *Metropolis*, one is struck by how many of their critical points and perspectives were already raised in the 20s, leaving the impression that Fritz Lang's film has both absorbed into itself and reflected back most of the responses it subsequently helped to provoke. Does this confirm that *Metropolis* is not quite the same kind of classic as *Hamlet* or *Ulysses*, where successive interpretations plumb new depths of meaning in works of infinite scope and inexhaustible richness of design? Probably yes, but as I have tried to indicate, *Metropolis* is also not quite their low-culture opposite: shallow and superficial, kitschy and 'deeply dishonest'.[99] If the most frequent judgment, ever since its Berlin opening, has been: 'great movie, shame about the story', this cannot be the whole truth, seeing how many 'readings' the story has by itself provoked. The pot-pourri of motifs may well have been opportunist and calculating, gathering up many pseudo-philosophical, social-romantic, decadent-dystopic clichés that in the 20s were 'in the air'. Yet despite this apparently self-inflicted handicap, von Harbou's plotting and Lang's visualisation must have structured these banal and sentimental commonplaces in ways that successfully imparted the illusion if not exactly of 'depth' then of archetypal resonance, reaching down into shared sensibilities and widely-felt anxieties as only myths and fairy-tales tend to do. There, it was the eclectic-encyclopaedic scope of the film that made it such fertile ground also for the postmodern fantasies it has subsequently inspired, putting it at some distance from the mostly disapproving scholarly analyses. Their U-turns in the course of time as well as the anachronisms cheerfully risked by pop appropriations suggest that any critical (ideological, political, gender-based) reading misses its target, pushing in open doors that only lead into more echo chambers of cultural-historical received ideas. In the Rorschach test that the film appears to have become, it is no longer *Metropolis*, but its critics that have come to look, if not incoherent, then somehow selective in their evidence and arbitrary in their assumptions.

Faced with the commercial, critical, archival and performative afterlives of *Metropolis*, one is tempted to conclude that this emblem of Weimar culture was not so much 'anticipating' postmodernism, as already taking a critical, self-critical but also perhaps, in the philospher Peter Sloterdijk's sense 'cynical' view of postmodernism. For it displays a kind of relativising 'knowledge' about itself that must affect all 'ideological' critiques of Lang's film, some of which would seem to 'have remained more naive than the ideology they set out to unmask'.[100] They turn the interpretations, along with Moroder's adaptation and Ridley Scott's, Tim Burton's or Terry Gilliam's pastiche appropriations, into mere 'extension' of Lang and von Harbou's work, projected into

Madonna, 'Express Yourself'
(Sire Records Company)

Queen, 'Radio Gaga' (Queen
Films Ltd/EMI Records Ltd)

(reception) history. Writing about *Metropolis* one cannot help feeling that one becomes yet another of Fritz Lang's pre-programmed 'ready-mades', to take up a phrase which Marcel Duchamp – another modernist of 'cynical reason' – once applied, only half in jest, not only to his *found objets*, but to the efforts of his more assiduous archivists, gallerists and tea-leaves reading interpreters. The 'rocker' Fritz Lang, after first 'turning in his grave' at the sight of Moroder, Bowie, Madonna or Freddie Mercury strutting their stuff and striking a pose, might be content to join in the fun. As the first and last man of Weimar cinema, he surely has the last laugh also on modernist critics, deconstructivists and postmodern pasticheurs alike: so far, it seems that *Metropolis* is still leading the field, with Lang always already back from where we are heading.

APPENDIX:
TELLING AND RETELLING 'METROPOLIS'
. . . .

Since few classic films have had quite so dramatic a textual and critical history as *Metropolis*, any telling of its story is necessarily a re-telling: what the first-night audience saw is not what subsequent viewers were able to see, for reasons given above, and yet it is important to attempt the most likely synopsis of the narrative and its logic as it might have been understood by the Berlin premiere audience, rather than to have recourse to von Harbou's novel. The consequence of cutting scenes in the Paramount version was that the plot had to be rearranged. What follows is based on the restored Munich version, with the text in square brackets referring to scenes presumed to have existed in the first-night Berlin version.

Prelude: Vertical arrows of light stamp onto the screen the title: 'Metropolis'. A cityscape, made up of towering skyscrapers, is incessantly caressed by shafts of light pointing upwards and playing across the buildings' massive contours. In Moroder's version, it is the year AD 2026, in the Paramount version, AD 3000. Pistons, shaped like ziggurats, move up and down, giving way to crankshafts and cogwheels, while connecting rods pushed by giant flywheels let machine parts rotate in the steady rhythm of a pounding mechanical heart. No human hand or figure is either visible or necessary: a *perpetuum mobile* made of gleaming steel seems to set the pace and dictate the speed at which the world of Metropolis lives and breathes. A ten-hour wall clock indicates that another shift is about to come to an end, with an organ-sized steam whistle out in the open blowing the signal in all four directions against the sky. Lined up in columns of ten or twelve abreast, bent and cowed workers in dark-blue overalls and tight-fitting black caps shuffle towards the lifts to take them down to their living quarters, while another, identical column moves in step along the tunnel to take over. As the steel cages glide down vertical shafts that resemble a mine, the camera has joined the throng of workers, gliding down with them, just long enough to impart its movement to the intertitles, also floating from the top of the screen to the bottom and describing the topography of the Workers' City now coming into view. Squat cubes, several storeys high, without access to sun or fresh air, they are grouped around a central square in which a giant gong is mounted on a pedestal. Still in formation, the workers gradually part on either side and disappear in the direction of the brightly-lit doorways, listing the inhabitants by five-digit numbers.

High above the machines and the workers' tenements is the 'Club of the sons' where the *jeunesse dorée* of Metropolis trains for an Olympic sprint in a huge open-air stadium lined with Greek statues. Winner of the race is Freder, son of Joh Fredersen, the master of Metropolis, soon after seen in the 'Eternal Gardens', an artificial grotto of exotic plants and strutting peacocks. This time, Freder is surrounded by lightly-clad ladies of the night, who chase him around a fountain rather than a cinder track. Suddenly the door at the far end opens and a ragged cluster of wide-eyed children emerges, led by a female figure dressed austerely in the Quaker style, blonde hair framing her face like a halo. The sight pierces Freder's heart like an arrow and, not for the last time, he clutches his breast. 'See', the saintly figure says to her flock, 'these are your brothers,' before being shooed back out. But Freder, one last glance at the artificial paradise of luscious vegetation and available flesh, rushes after the apparition. Unfamiliar with the nether worlds, he ends up in the machine rooms, where banks of workers manipulate levers, turn dials and man control panels. He sees a haggard worker on the brink of collapse. The machine under his command starts to overheat and eventually causes an explosion that kills scores of men flung through the air, and whose bodies are immediately carted away, while other workers take their place. Knocked briefly unconscious by the blast and deeply shocked by what he sees, Freder has a vision of the machine as man-eating Moloch, into whose fiery maw rows and rows of chained workers are tossed, as in Inca depictions of human sacrifices or a medieval Cathedral tympanum showing sinners entering purgatory (also, a screen memory of Pastrone's *Cabiria* (1913) and Griffith's *Intolerance* (1916)). Shielding his eyes from these horrors, Freder finally tears himself away and, reaching street level, boards a taxi that is to take him to the 'New Tower of Babel', Joh Fredersen's headquarters. In his father's magnificently appointed office with a picture window spanning one entire wall and overlooking the Metropolis skyline as far as the eye can see, Freder tells him about the dreadful conditions of the workers, but is rebuffed like the unwelcome intruder he is, and curtly lectured about the necessity of each class to keep to its proper place. Freder realises that his father is more concerned about security and surveillance than workers' safety when he sees him dismiss Josephat, his personal assistant, for having allowed his son to stray to the lower levels, but also because the foreman Grot, rather than Josephat, informs Fredersen about some mysterious drawings found on the dead workers. The foreman gone and Freder having rushed after Josephat, Fredersen instructs 'Slim' to keep his son under surveillance.[101] With Josephat, whom he has in the meantime dissuaded from committing suicide, as his accomplice, Freder returns to the machine room, where he takes over from another worker about to collapse at the controls. [Finding money in Freder's clothes, this worker, number 11811 who now remembers that he has a name, Georgy, is transfixed by the sight of a semi-naked female figure in the car pulling up alongside his at an intersection. Instead of following Freder's instructions to wait for him at Josephat's house, he heads straight for Yoshiwara, the city's exclusive night club. 'Slim', unaware of the identity switch, follows Georgy thinking it is Freder.]

Brooding over the incident and disturbed by the maps found circulating among the workers, Fredersen goes to see his former rival in love and power, Rotwang. The scientific brain behind Metropolis, he is now a recluse inventor – half medieval magus, half R&D man of a multinational conglomerate – working on a robot-replica of Hel, the woman he had lost to Fredersen. [The two have a heated exchange in front of a giant bust of Hel that Fredersen discovers behind a curtain in Rotwang's house. Raising his artificial hand in a gesture of triumph, Rotwang predicts that soon the robot woman will bear the features of Hel: 'She'll be mine again, Fredersen, and you can keep her son!'] Flattered by Fredersen's admission of helplessness, when he tells him about the reason for his visit, Rotwang deciphers the plans and promises to take Fredersen to the workers' meeting in the catacombs. In the meantime, Freder has been labouring on Georgy's machine, barely able to keep up with the flashing lights and heavy pointers. Now a worker among workers, Freder is literally crucified on the giant dial, crying out: 'Father, I never knew ten hours could last such an eternity!' Released at last, he follows his fellow workers to their clandestine assembly-point. There he discovers that the girl he has fallen in love with is none other than Maria, the workers' spiritual leader. She tells them the parable of the Tower of Babel, built by slaves, but also destroyed by them, because no common language existed between the rulers and the ruled. Freder's and Maria's eyes meet as she promises them the advent of a saviour: 'mediator between brain and hand has to be the heart.' This scene is witnessed by Rotwang and Joh Fredersen from a raised platform in the recess of the catacombs. [Only Rotwang has recognised Freder among the workers. Suddenly seized by a diabolical plan of revenge,] Rotwang agrees to kidnap Maria, in order to give the robot her likeness and make her Joh Fredersen's agent provocateur, leading the workers in a self-destructive uprising, masterminded by the inventor. Freder stays behind to talk to Maria, who gives him a chaste kiss, as if to confirm his dawning resolve to become the longed-for mediator. They arrange to meet again at the Cathedral the next day. With Freder as well as Fredersen gone, Rotwang traps Maria in the beam of his flashlight and manages to chase her along the underground passages right into his house.

As this plot-point makes clear, the film as originally conceived possessed an added dimension – enfolding a past into the story's present, that of the lethal battle of the fathers, now fought out on the backs of the 'son' and 'daughter'. Lang's *Metropolis*, like his *Die Nibelungen* – anticipating *Rancho Notorious*, from which the phrase is taken – is a tale of 'hate, murder and revenge'. The triad acerbically balances the parable of recognition, forgiveness and redemption emphasised by von Harbou in her novel, and against her Catholic faith, it pits the Hellenic pathos of tragedy, or the more archaic law of the blood-feud. But the narrative also becomes rather more comparable to a struggle for power over several generations, centred on the connection of business and sexuality, present rivalry and old wrongs, private empires and the exchange of women, itself an ambiguous celebration of corporate capitalism's power to divide and join, separate and recombine: a process of which the fragmented and recycled, re-edited and reassembled prints of *Metropolis* seem an appropriately self-referential as well as self-consuming instance.

Intermezzo: The next day Freder goes to the Cathedral, the first time we see this strangely soaring and yet diminished building incongruously surviving among the high-rises that surround it. Freder cannot find Maria anywhere. [Instead, he comes across an Anabaptist monk, preaching the apocalypse and the coming of the whore of Babylon. Cross-cut to Rotwang, putting the final touches to his experiment, muttering ominously to his robot that she will destroy Joh Fredersen, his son and the city.] Searching for Maria, Freder contemplates a bas-relief depicting the Grim Reaper and the Seven Deadly Sins. Still under the impact of the hellfire sermon, he kneels to pray. [Cut to Georgy, leaving the Yoshiwara night club after his debauches, having lost all of Freder's money. 'Slim' is waiting for him and bundles him into the car, forcing him to confess that he was supposed to meet Josephat and Freder at the latter's home. Cut to Freder, on his way to meet Josephat, and expecting there to find Georgy who is to establish the contact with the workers' secret association. But threatened by 'Slim', Georgy immediately returns to his machine to work a shift. 'Slim' turns up at Josephat's house, but Freder has already left. He tries to bribe Josephat into leaving town, not least to hush up his own mistake, but Josephat refuses and the two men start a fight. Josephat is knocked unconscious and locked into a room.] Cut to Rotwang, who has just drugged Maria unconscious and dragged her into his lab. Wandering the streets [in Moroder's version: leaving the Church], Freder passes Rotwang's sinister abode and thinks he can hear cries for help from the captive Maria. Forcing his way in, he is himself trapped by Rotwang and cannot prevent the creation of her double. In a spectacular scene, unleashing Faustian powers and a Frankensteinian 'tent of electricity' (Paul Jensen), Rotwang succeeds in transferring the traits of Maria (encased in a sarcophagus like an Egyptian pharaoh or the glass-coffin of Sleeping Beauty) to the steel monster sitting on a raised throne in front of a pentagram. Freder finally wakes from his swoon and challenges Rotwang, who tells him that Maria has gone to see his father. [There, she hands Fredersen an envelope in which Rotwang invites the master of Metropolis to a gala evening at his house.] Freder surprises Maria in his father's arms and, not realising that it is the robot with Maria's traits, comes down with brain fever. He has to be taken home and is briefly visited by his father, who accidentally leaves behind the invitation. At Rotwang's soirée, during a magnificent floor-show, a jewel box carried by black slaves opens up to reveal a lascivious Maria, her body contoured in a costume of sheer light, dancing provocatively before a sea of devouring eyes. Or is it merely Freder's fever-brained nightmare vision, imagining the seductive-destructive whore of Babylon? 'Slim', left by Fredersen at Freder's bedside [turns briefly into the Monk from the Cathedral]. At Rotwang's reception, the sight of the false Maria whips two men into a sexual frenzy. Blasphemously they vow to commit all seven deadly sins for her sake. Freder fantasises the Cathedral bas-relief coming to life and threateningly marching towards him, the Grim Reaper out front.

Here, the cross-threading of the plot and its sub-plots – the failure of 'Slim's surveillance mission and the failure of Josephat's protection of Freder – asymmetrically mirror each other, just as the desperate attempts of Maria to escape from Rotwang's house through a skylight are inversely repeated when Freder attempts in vain to enter Rotwang's house in response to her shouts. The complex pattern of alternations induces in the viewer the sort of suspended animation that also seizes Freder and plunges him into fever-dreams. From then on to the end of the intermezzo, subjective projection and objective incident remain indistinguishable, the Yoshiwara sexual whirlwind raging in Freder's mind as much as the Cathedral dance of death.

Furioso: Nursed back to health, Freder learns about the existence of Maria's double from Josephat, who has gone underground, disguising himself as a worker. ['Slim' reports to Fredersen about the false Maria preaching rebellion to the workers, while Josephat reports to Freder about the madness that has overcome his erstwhile friends in the 'Club of the Sons'.] Jan and Marinus challenge each other to a duel, in which one dies and the other is shot that very same evening by another man, all because of Maria. The sirens of Metropolis announce another shift-change, and Freder returns to the catacombs, expecting to find Maria, but it is the false Maria who now incites the workers to wait no more for the mediator, and smash the machines. [Fredersen, in the meantime, has given instructions not to obstruct the workers should they revolt, while Rotwang, who still holds the true Maria captive, tells her about his own instruction to the false Maria.] In the catacombs, one of the workers recognises Freder and 'outs' him as Fredersen's son, whereupon the workers try to lynch him. Georgy and Josephat try to protect Freder, and Georgy receives a fatal stab-wound. In the ensuing mêlée, Freder and Josephat escape, while the workers surge forward towards the 'heart machine'. [Fredersen, having returned to Rotwang for advice, overhears him confessing his scheme to Maria. He knocks Rotwang down, and while the men fight, Maria manages to escape.]

The workers, led by the false Maria, have reached the iron gates, tear them down and start storming the machines.[102] The foreman makes contact with Fredersen via a televisual intercom, but inexplicably, he is once more told to let the workers have their way. Grot, sensing a plot, opposes the mob single-handedly and starts to reason with the workers, to no avail. Spurred on by Maria, they sabotage the heart-machine. Wildly dancing the 'Carmagnole' of revolutionary destruction, they do not notice the false Maria stealing herself away. Cut to the real Maria, wandering through the abandoned Worker's City, suddenly aware that things are not well, as elevators crash down around her and water slowly forces its way through the concrete floors. She rushes to the homes, calls the children and gathers them together in the central square, where they climb the plinth on which is mounted the giant gong, which Maria desperately tries to activate in order to summon help. Only Josephat and Freder respond and come to her aid, but as the water is rising inexorably, a skylight grate blocks their exit and only at the last minute can they all make their escape to the upper city and shepherd the charges into 'Club of the Sons'. Below, in the machine rooms, as if waking from a trance, the workers realise too late the danger to their children: grief-stricken, they become a lynch mob, charging after 'the witch who is responsible for it all'. The false Maria, having returned to the Yoshiwara Club, calls for a witches' sabbath. Leading the revellers down into the streets, she shouts: 'let's watch the world go to hell!' while from the machine rooms below, an angry crowd has gathered to find Maria in the upper city. The two masses of people clash, and the workers manage to catch Maria and drag her in front of the Cathedral where a hastily gathered pile is ready for the witch to be burnt at the stake.

Fredersen, in the meantime, has learnt that his son is still in the Workers' City and likely to drown with the rest. [Rotwang has recovered consciousness, but seems to have gone mad. He drags himself in front of the statue of Hel, promising to bring her home at last.] Freder [having lost sight of Maria in a scuffle with the workers] reaches the Cathedral Square and watches in horror, unaware that it is the false Maria who is tied to the stake. Inside the Cathedral, Rotwang is pursuing the real Maria whom he believes to be the robot Maria, chasing her up the bell tower and onto the roof. As the flames outside consume the stake, the writhing figure turns into the steel robot, and Freder suddenly catches sight of Rotwang carrying the limp and faint Maria on his back along the Cathedral parapet. He rushes after them, just as Fredersen, accompanied by Josephat and 'Slim', also arrives in front of the Cathedral. The workers threaten Fredersen, but

Josephat assures them that their children are safe thanks to Freder, whom everyone now watches fighting with Rotwang high up, silhouetted against the night sky. Slipping on the pitched roof, Rotwang falls to his death while Freder manages to pull Maria to safety. On the steps in front of the main gate, Maria beckons Freder and Fredersen. The workers, once more in formation and headed by Grot, advance towards the group. Taking his father's hand, Freder moves towards the foreman who is eventually prepared to shake hands with his boss, the heart as mediator joining head and hand. Industrial peace and the status quo have returned, but Fredersen's city lies in ruins and Rotwang has taken to his death the secret of artificial life.

Across the double plot-line of the two Marias, the fairy-tale romance and the family drama of the succession of generations, an ebb and flow of contending masses carry the motif of the rising flood into the realm of human agents, with the individual protagonists alternately separating from and fusing with the masses. Lower city and upper city, Cathedral Square and burning stake, bell tower and roof-top provide the successive stages on which the action mounts to its crescendo, before Rotwang's fatal plunge lowers the temperature, and the dawn light cools down the general intoxication. So perfectly choreographed are these tidal motions and synchronised with the rise and fall of the film's emotional fever-chart that the political implications of the closing gesture are left open. The end balances several formal patterns, but in the story world, they resolve little and explain even less. The acrid smell of destruction and the taste of exhaustion linger in the early morning air.

NOTES

. . . .

1 This description is from a Lang interview first published in *Focus on Film* in 1975, and repeated in Peter Bogdanovich's interview book, *Fritz Lang in America*. Lang took it almost verbatim from an article he wrote in January 1925 about his first trip to the States for *Film-Kurier*, a leading trade publication. Since then, book after book has repeated the story, from Siegfried Kracauer to Paul Jensen, from Alfred Eibel to Frederic Ott. At the last count, more than a dozen articles or chapters on *Metropolis* open with this passage.

2 Wolfgang Jacobsen (ed.), *Erich Pommer* (Berlin: Argon, 1989), p. 70.

3 Ann Drummond, *Fritz Lang's Metropolis*, unpublished M.Phil. dissertation, University of Edinburgh, 1982, pp. 8–9.

4 Textual comparison indicates that some rewriting took place between the instalments (from August 1926 onwards) and the published novel (January 1927). Since shooting of the film had started in May 1925, there must have been a completed screenplay, suggesting that the novel came both *before* and *after* the screenplay. Leonardo Quaresima argues that the instalment version was written after the shooting script, but that the novel preceded the writing of the script. Quaresima, 'Ninon, la hermana de Maria. Metropolis y sus variantes', *Archivos de la Filmoteca de Valencia* vol. 17, June 1994, pp. 5–7.

5 There was a translation into English (1928) and also a novelisation in French, written by Alain Laubreaux and Serge Plaute (Paris: Gallimard, 1928).

6 Reinhold Keiner, *Thea von Harbou und der Deutsche Film bis 1933* (Hildesheim: Georg Olms, 1984), pp. 191 and 193.

7 Paul M. Jensen, 'Metropolis – the Film and the Book', in *Metropolis: A Film by Fritz Lang* (London: Lorrimer, 1973), pp. 5–14. For a more detailed comparison, based on newly available evidence, see Quaresima, 'Ninon, la hermana de Maria', pp. 5–37.

8 An exception is Paul Coates who provides a sympathetic reading of von Harbou's contribution in *The Gorgon's Gaze* (Cambridge: Cambridge University Press, 1991), pp. 41–52.

9 Anon., 'Claims Metropolis Play', *New York Times*, 23 December 1928 mentions a plagiarism suit against UFA, Pommer and von Harbou. For von Harbou's debt to Georg Kaiser, see also Barry Salt, 'From Caligari to Who?', *Sight and Sound*, Spring 1979, pp. 119–23.

10 Kurt Pinthus, 'Lemberg und Metropolis', *Das Tagebuch* vol. 8 no. 3, 15 January 1917, p. 99.

11 '[It] is not life […], but, pardon the expression, fashionable ladies' home journal romanticism.' Willy Haas, 'Zwei große Filmpremieren', *Die Literarische Welt* vol. 3 no.3, 21 January 1927, p. 7.

12 Luis Buñuel, 'Metropolis', *La Gazeta Literaria*, 1 May 1927.

13 See also Jean Epstein's and Blaise Cendrar's reviews, cited in Richard Abel, *French Cinema: The First Wave* (Princeton: Princeton University Press, 1988).

14 'Deux erreurs: Metropolis, Princess Masha', *Les Annales*, 15 November 1927, n.p.

15 'The main thesis was Thea von Harbou's, but I'm at least 50% responsible, because I directed the film. At the time, I wasn't as political as I am now. One cannot make a politically conscious film by claiming that the heart mediates between the hand and the brain – that's a fairy-tale, really. I was more interested in machines …' Peter Bogdanovich, *Fritz Lang in America* (London: Studio Vista, 1967), p. 124. See also Jean Domarchi and Jacques Rivette, 'Entretien avec Fritz Lang', *Cahiers du cinéma* vol. 99, September 1959.

16 Lang had a very public affair with Gerda Maurus, his leading lady in *Spione* (1928), and in 1932, von Harbou met Ayi Tendulkar, who became her permanent companion. Lang and von Harbou's marriage was officially dissolved on 26 April 1933. Von Harbou's comment: 'we were married eleven years, because for ten years we were too busy to get a divorce.' Quoted in Keiner, *Thea von Harbou*, p. 303.

17 There are scores of reviews, including H. G. Wells' diatribe, detailing how nonsensical, old-fashioned or ignorant of science the gadgets, machines and industrial facilities in the film are. H. G. Wells, 'Metropolis – The Silliest Film Ever Made', *New York Times*, 17 April

1927; Axel Eggebrecht, 'Technik, Arbeit und Wissenschaft der Zukunft: Möglichkeiten eines Zukunftfilms', *Kulturwille* vol 4. no. 6, 1927, pp. 123–5.

18 One of Lang's subsequent projects, *Die Frau im Mond* is in this respect the counterpart: very precise in its technical details about rocket propulsion and the science of space travel. See Guntram Geser, *Fritz Lang, Metropolis und Die Frau im Mord* (Meitingen: Corian, 1996), p. 11.

19 'Eucharastic and thomistic,/ and besides a bit marxistic,/ theosophic, communistic,/ gothic-small town-abbey-mystic,/ activistic, arch-buddhistic,/ far-east wise and taoistic,/ seeking in the negro-sculpture/salvation from the Zeitgeist-culture,/ raising voice and barricade,/ God and foxtrott have it made [...] [my translation]. Franz Werfel, 'Spiegelmensch' (1920), quoted in Fred Gehler and Ullrich Kasten (eds), *Fritz Lang: die Stimme von Metropolis* (Berlin: Hensehel, 1990), p. 43.

20 This build-up of pressure was well perceived at the time. One reviewer described the film as '[t]he vision of a world shortly before midnight, the dance on a volcano, a minute before it erupts'. E. S. P., 'Metropolis', *Licht-Bild-Bühne*, 11 January 1927.

21 Theodor Heuss, 'Metropolis', *Die Hilfe* vol. 33 no. 4, 15 February 1927, p. 109.

22 E. S. P., 'Metropolis'.

23 'If I imagine that one of these dead chessboard figures [in the film] might actually read a book that I have myself standing in the bookshelf, then the whole clockwork mechanism of this artificial work seizes up, because it does not bear even the slightest contact with palpable reality.' Willy Haas, 'Zwei große Filmpremieren'.

24 Roland Schacht [Balthasar], 'Der Metropolisfilm', *Das Blaue Heft* vol. 9 no. 3, 1 February 1927, p. 74.

25 Heide Schönemann, *Fritz Lang: Filmbilder Vorbilder* (Berlin: Hentrich, 1992), pp. 76–7.

26 Otto Hunte (1881–1947). His art direction credits include, apart from most major Lang films from the 1920s, *The Blue Angel* (Joseph von Sternberg, 1930) and *Jew Süss* (Veit Harlan, 1940). After the war, he worked in East Germany for DEFA. Erich Kettelhut

(1893–1979) did art direction on films of Joe May, Fritz Lang, Hanns Schwarz, Robert Siodmak and Georg Jacoby. He also stayed in Germany throughout the Nazi period, and worked again with Lang on *The Thousand Eyes of Dr Mabuse* (1960).

27 Erich Kettelhut, *Erinnerungen*, unpublished memoir, Stiftung Deutsche Kinemathek, Berlin. It is an acknowledged source in Patrick McGilligan's chapter on *Metropolis* in *Fritz Lang: The Nature of the Beast* (New York: St. Martin's Press, 1997), pp. 108–33.

28 Günther Rittau, 'Die Trickaufnahmen im Metropolis Film', *Die Filmtechnik*, 28 January 1927. See also Lang's own description of the different special effects, in 'La Nuit Viennoise', *Cahiers du cinéma* vol. 169, August 1965 and vol. 179, June 1966.

29 After a complaint by a delegation of extras about the cold, Lang ordered his assistant to distribute ten bottles of brandy. Alfred Abel, the actor playing Joh Fredersen, tells about gallantly rescuing an extra shivering in a flimsy evening dress by lending her his coat. 'Der Schauspieler hat das Wort', *Ufa Magazin Sondernummer Metropolis*, 14 January 1927.

30 Gustav Fröhlich, *Waren das Zeiten: Mein Film-Heldenleben* (Munich: Herbig, 1982).

31 Thea von Harbou, 'Wie schreibt man Filmmanuskripte? - Die ersten Bilder von Metropolis', *Berliner Tageblatt* vol. 489, 16 October 1926; Thea von Harbou, *Ufa Magazin, Sondernummer Metropolis*, January 1927; Thea von Harbou, 'Aus dem Metropolis Manuskript', *Presse und Propaganda-Heft Metropolis* Berlin, 1927; Thea von Harbou-Lang, 'Metropolis', in Kurt Mühsam (ed.), *Film und Kino* (1927).

32 The widely varying figures given as the film's final cost reflect the odd accounting habits of UFA, before it was reorganised in 1927/8 by Ludwig Klitzsch. Although evidently a very expensive film, it is also clear that, in subsequent litigation with Lang, UFA debited the *Metropolis* production with all kinds of studio overheads, including part of the cost for the other superproduction of 1925/6, Murnau's *Faust*. See Drummond, *Fritz Lang's Metropolis*, p. 9.

33 Klaus Kreimeier, 'Hohlraum und Bauhütte', in *Die Ufa Story* (Munich: Hanser, 1992), pp. 115–32.

34 R. Giesen, 'Special Effects made in Germany'. See also Helmut Weihsmann, Gebaute Illusionen: Architektur im Film (Vienna: Promedia, 1988), pp. 146–9.

35 See the *Ufa Magazin, Sondernummer Metropolis*, 14 January 1927, which features more than a dozen articles by the director, screenwriter, cinematographer, art director and actors. Essays on the technical aspects of *Metropolis* also appeared in early 1927 in the trade journals *Filmtechnik, Die Filmwoche* and *Der Kinematograph*.

36 Curt Siodmak, *Unter Wolfsmenschen* (Bonn: Weidle, 1995), pp. 107–10.

37 The extras playing the Egyptian slaves were taken from the Berlin dole queue not because actors were not prepared to shave their heads (one can see on stills that some of the slaves are not shaven), but because UFA could claim back from their wages a tax discount (see also the contract reproduced in the press-and-propaganda book).

38 Willy Haas opened his review with 'Already a year and a half now, word of mouth has it that here one of the seven wonders of the world is being created.' After enumerating all the statistics, he concludes sarcastically: 'Not much [for a world wonder] – don't laugh, dear Reader.' Haas, 'Zwei große Filmpremieren'.

39 The *Film-Journal*, 14 January 1927, gave a blow-by-blow account of the opening night under the first-page banner headline '"Metropolis" – the Biggest German Film', so did the *New York Times*: 'Metropolis Film Seen. Berlin witnesses a Grim Portrayal of Industrial Future', 10 January 1927, p. 36.

40 Owing to the many cues written into the score, the Huppertz music still provides one of the most accurate indications of the narrative sequence of the first release version. Of the gramophone record ('sole rights Vox-Company'), which is advertised in the *Licht-Bild-Bühne*, 15 January 1927, only one copy is known to have survived in a private collection. Its owner apparently refuses to sell it, lend it out, or even play it to visitors, for fear

of secret copying. My thanks to Martin Koerber for this information.

41 'Characterstic of the film-manufacturers' lack of instinct is their desire to transform into a quality product the subject matter of colportage. Things that breathe in pamphlet form suffocate in polished leather bindings. This is literally true: on *Spione*'s opening night, critics were handed a volume that was a marvel of the art of bookbinding and that contained nothing more than Thea von Harbou's novel.' Siegfried Kracauer, 'Film 1928', in *The Mass Ornament* (Cambridge, MA: Harvard University Press, 1995), pp. 316–17.

42 The front-of-house decorations were a specialty of UFA's resident architect Rudi Feld, famous for his huge displays on the UFA-Palast am Zoo, a drab-looking neo-Gothic brick affair when 'undressed' during the day, but at night and with the lights on, a magic citadel of architectural folly promising fabulous fantasies. For *Metropolis*, the entire UFA-Pavilion at the Nollendorfplatz, where the film had its Berlin run, was covered with a special silver paint that made it shimmer at night, lit from below with powerful footlights, while over the entrance was mounted a replica of the giant gong with which Maria warns the children of Metropolis of the imminent flood. See also Kreimeier, *Die Ufa Story*, pp. 133–46.

43 This was the view of Fred Hildenbrandt, 'Metropolis', *Berliner Tageblatt*, 11 January 1927, and of Herman G. Scheffauer, 'An Impression of the German Film Metropolis', *New York Times*, 6 March 1927, p. 7.

44 The only source recording this Vienna opening on 10 February 1927 is Bernard Eisenschitz, 'Metropolis, UFA et le cinéma allemand', in *Metropolis: Images d'un tournage* (Paris: Cinémathèque française, 1985), p. 142. Enno Patalas claims in an interview that the Berlin premiere version was also shown in Stettin (now: Gdinia, Poland) 'by accident'. See Lorenzo Codelli, 'Entretien avec Enno Patalas', *Positif* vol. 285, November 1984, pp. 12–20.

45 Prints of this British version have been identified in London (NFTVA) and in Melbourne (Harry Davidson).

46 *The Bioscope* vol. 70 no. 1966, 17 March 1927, and *The Bioscope* vol. 71 no. 1070, 14 April 1927: 'Now in its fourth week, acclaimed by Press and Public Alike as the Greatest Screen Achievement Ever Seen: *M*iraculous – *E*normous – *T*remendous – *R*emarkable – *O*verwhelming – *P*henomenal – *O*utstanding – *L*ucrative – *I*nstantaneous – *S*uccess'.

47 'Channing Pollock Gives His Impression of *Metropolis*', Paramount Press Kit for *Metropolis*, quoted in Martin Koerber, 'Notizen zur Überlieferung des Films *Metropolis*', in W. Jacobsen and W. Sudendorf (eds), *Metropolis. Aus dem Laboratorium der Filmischen Moderne* (Stuttgart: Edition Menges, 2000). As Welford Beaton sarcastically commented: 'a job that brought [Pollock] twenty-thousand dollars and his name in gigantic letters on the screen'. *The Film Spectator*, 3 September 1927.

48 'It is agreed that *Metropolis* will be restarted in the American version, after suitable removal of all intertitles with communist tendencies'. For a full discussion of the *Metropolis* case, see UFA file R 109, Bundesarchiv: Niederschrift der Vorstandssitzungen, vols 7, 8 and 27, April 1927. Also quoted in Kreimeier, *Die Ufa Story*, pp. 189–90.

49 Randolph Bartlett, 'German Film Revision Upheld as Needed Here', *New York Times*, 13 March 1927.

50 However, in a letter to Wolfgang Klaue, Head of the State Film Archive GDR from 1971, Lang vigorously denounces the Paramount version, but claims that his 'authorized' version ran two hours and five minutes, which is much closer in length to the second German release version than the premiere version, possibly implying that he had himself approved the cuts.

51 In 1988, the successor of UFA in West Germany, the Friedrich Wilhelm Murnau Stiftung came across thirty tins of *Metropolis* nitrate material, of which only five tins were copied to safety films and the rest detroyed. There is a tantalising but unsubstantiated rumour that these might have been the out-takes from the first release version. See Koerber, 'Notizen zur Überlieferung'.

52 Vincent Pinel has called such films 'oeuvres polymorphes', adding directorial intervention, as in the case of Gance, to the usual commercial considerations of distributors and the interference of the censors. 'Pour une déontologie de la restauration des films', *Positif* vol. 421, March 1996, p. 90.

53 Martin Koerber, to whom I owe much of this information, discusses the dilemmas arising from this practice for the film-restorer, when having to decide between near-identical scenes. See Koerber, 'Notizen zur Überlieferung'.

54 Roland Schacht [Balthasar], 'Der Metropolis Film', p. 76.

55 This thought occurred to me after interviewing my mother about her cinema-going habits in Wiesbaden (a provincial spa near Frankfurt) in the late 20s. She had heard of *Metropolis* but never seen it, saying 'it probably never did come to our local cinema, and at the [Wiesbaden] Ufa-Palast it just was too expensive for me.' She did, however, clearly remember seeing and hearing Al Jolson in *The Singing Fool* (1928) and *Sonny Boy* (1929).

56 A detailed account – in parts, reading like a Le Carré Cold War thriller – is given by Martin Koerber of the origins and fate of these prints. See Koerber, 'Notizen zur Überlieferung'. Enno Patalas has also published a very useful chronology and described his own odyssey with the film. See Enno Patalas, 'Metropolis – Die Zukunftsstadt – ein Trümmerfilm', in Irmbert Schenk (ed.), *Dschungel Großstadt. Kino und Modernisierung* (Marburg: Schüren, 1999).

57 Jahnke also compiled a detailed restoration report, which now constitutes an important documentary source for all subsequent archival projects and scholarship. 'Handakte zur Rekonstruktion von *Metropolis*', Bundesarchiv-Filmarchiv, Berlin.

58 See Giorgio Bertellini, 'Restoration, Genealogy and Palimpsests. On Some Historiographical Questions', *Film History* vol. 7 no. 3, Autumn 1995, p. 281.

59 On the Munich version, see Enno Patalas, 'Metropolis, Scene 103', *Camera Obscura* vol. 15, 1986, pp. 165–73 and also his 'Metropolis – Die Zukunftsstadt – ein Trümmerfilm', pp. 15–28.

60 Frédéric Vitoux, 'Un rocker nommé Fritz Lang', *Nouvel Observateur*, 6 July 1984. The article also features an interview with Gustav Fröhlich, who shows himself 'delighted' by the new version.

61 See Raymond Bellour, 'On Fritz Lang', in Stephen Jenkins (ed.), *Fritz Lang, the Image and the Look* (London: British Film Institute, 1981), pp. 26–37.

62 Katja Hink, 'Der Film ist sein Schicksal. Peter Franz restauriert *Metropolis*', *Wiesbadener Kurier*, 18 September 1999, p. 2.

63 Koerber, 'Notizen zur Überlieferung'.

64 See especially the reviews of Siemsen, Ickes, Haas, Jhering, Heuss, listed in the Bibliography.

65 Felix Ziege, 'Metropolis und wir', *Kulturwille* vol. 4 no. 6, 1927, p. 125.

66 Cited in Drummond, *Fritz Lang's Metropolis*, p. 155. Drummond sees the politics of the film closest to the 'centrist' position within the Weimar parliamentary spectrum, linking it to the DDP, which was in alliance with the ruling Social Democrats.

67 Siegfried Hartmann, 'Metropolis-Technik', *Deutsche Allgemeine Zeitung*, 20 January 1927.

68 Theodor Heuss shrewdly observed that Lang had simply taken the backstairs/front house opposition of the Expressionist 'Kammerspielfilm' and turned it 90 degrees into the vertical. Heuss, 'Metropolis'.

69 Otto Kriegk, *Der deutsche Film im Spiegel der Ufa. 25 Jahre Kampf und Vollendung* (Berlin: Ufa-Buchverlag, 1943), pp. 88–9.

70 Siegfried Kracauer, *From Caligari to Hitler* (Princeton: Princeton University Press, 1947), p. 149.

71 Enno Patalas to the author, Bremen, December 1998.

72 On 30 December 1931, a headline in the (pro-Nazi) *Sachsenhäuser Anzeiger* derided a number of modernist high-rise projects planned by the social-democrat mayor and city council, under the title 'A Narrow Escape: Ludwig Landmann's Metropolis in Frankfurt'.

73 Unidentified review, clipping file *Metropolis*, British Film Institute.

74 As with the Tower of Babel parable, Moloch refers to a passage in Leviticus xviii, 21.

75 The image reappears rather too literally in Alan Parker's *Pink Floyd The Wall*, where the scene already quoted ends with the schoolchildren falling into a meat-grinder.

76 Georges Sadoul, *Histore de l'art du cinéma des origines à nos jours* (Paris: Flammarion, 1966), p. 156. From Sadoul's account it is not clear whether this recognition refers to Lang's film as a warning or a model. The passage is also cited by Claude-Jean Phillipe, 'Analyse d'un grand film: Metropolis', *Télérama*, 24 October 1965, pp. 79–80 and his 'La terrible co-existence de toutes choses', in Eisenschitz (ed.), *Metropolis Images d'un tournage*, p. 9.

77 Thomas Pynchon, *Gravity's Rainbow* (New York: Bantam Books, 1972), p. 674. Rudolf Klein-Rogge (Thea von Harbou's first husband), it will be remembered, is not only Rotwang the scientist in *Metropolis*, but also played Lang's Dr Mabuse, his Attila the Hun in *Die Nibelungen* and Haghi the master spy in *Spione*.

78 The most sustained readings in this vein were those by Roger Dadoun ('*Metropolis*, Mère-Cité, Mittler, Hitler', *Revue Française de Psychanalyse*, January 1974 [in English: *Camera Obscura* vol.15, 1986, pp. 137–64]), Patricia Mellencamp ('Oedipus and the Robot in *Metropolis*', *Enclitic* vol. 5 no. 1, Spring 1981, pp. 20–42) and Andreas Huyssen ('The Vamp and the Machine: Technology and Sexuality in Fritz Lang's Metropolis', *New German Critique* vol. 24 no. 25, Fall/Winter 1981/2, pp. 221–37), to which must be added an archival-philological essay by Georges Sturm ('Für Hel ein Denkmal,', *Bulletin in Cicim* vol. 9, 1984) on the significance of the central figure of Hel, as an allusion to Nordic sagas.

79 Rudolf Arnheim would have disagreed: 'Not a trace of *Neue Sachlichkeit*. Instead of letting the sober-hygienic spirit of technology blow some fresh air through this soul, the snob Fritz Lang got his inspiration for two years' worth of work from the most philistine art salons.' 'Metropolis', *Das Stachelschwein*, 1 February 1927, p. 53.

80 Anton Kaes, 'Cinema and Modernity: On Fritz Lang's *Metropolis*', in R. Grimm and J.

Hermand (eds), *High and Low. German Attempts at Mediation* (Madison: University of Wisconsin Press, 1994), pp. 32–3.

81 In *Blade Runner*, it is the Freder figure, rather than Maria, who is doubled, as Deckard and Roy Batty both seek to meet their 'maker', the Master of the Tyrell Corporation. Rotwang is the more benevolent wizard J. F. Sebastian, and Maria has become the 'perfect' replicant Rachel, with whom Deckard finally flees to the Outer Worlds, an ending also first imagined by von Harbou for *Metropolis*, but finally rejected. For a detailed analysis, see Scott Bukatman, *Blade Runner* (London: British Film Institute, 1998).

82 Erich Kettelhut, 'Es wird anders gebaut', *Filmtechnik* vol. 16, 3 August 1929, p. 339.

83 Among the horrified gasps were those of Claude Beylie. See 'Dédales de Metropolis', *Cinématographe*, July 1984, p. 24.

84 *Metropolis*, the Musical, produced by Michael White, directed by Jerome Savary, with music by Joe Brooks, text and lyrics by Dusty Hughes and Joe Brooks, opened at the Piccadilly Theatre London on 1 March 1989. It was an expensive flop, despite Ralph Koltai's 'breathtaking sets' which included 'three-storey mammoth machines and elevators' as well as 'successful choral parts with lots of brass and sythesiser' amidst the 'all too Lloyd-Webberish compositions'. Julian Exner, 'Klassenkampf mit Musik', *Frankfurter Rundschau*, 5 April 1989.

85 'For the centenary of the cinema, a jazz trio from the Rhein-Main area has written a new musical accompaniment for the silent classic *Metropolis*. […] On stage are Colin Dunwoddie (sax, flute), Ernst Seitz (piano) and Silvia Sauer (vocals), stylistically moving between Modern Jazz and Avant-garde. In contrast to the pop-version of Giorgio Moroder, the trio does not use electronic instruments. Its chamber music arrangement maintains a deliberate distance from the 70-year-old sci-fi film, considered controversial because of its proximity to national-socialist thinking.' *Filmecho/Filmwoche*, July 1975, p. 11.

86 Michael Althen, 'Kunst im Bau', *Süddeutsche Zeitung*, 26 October 1988.

87 Unsigned press item, *Berlinale Journal*, 13 February 1992.

88 It is under this title that I initially reviewed the Moroder version for the *Monthly Film Bulletin* vol. 59 no. 611, December 1984, pp. 366–7.

89 Walter Benjamin, 'Unpacking My Library', in *Illuminations* (New York: Schocken Books, 1968), p. 67.

90 Paul Ickes, 'Metropolis', *Die Filmwoche* vol. 3, 19 January 1927, p. 60.

91 'This film is a geometrical film – the first step on the way to the abstract film.' *Film-Journal*, 14 January 1927, p. 1.

92 Quoted in Kreimeier, *Die Ufa Story*, p.18.

93 Martin Koerber suggests the machine might control the lifts and elevators that one sees crash so spectacularly later in the film (verbal communication).

94 Manfred Etten, 'Aber ich interessierte mich für Maschinen…', *Film-Dienst* vol. 45 no. 1, 7 January 1992, p. 38.

95 Neumann, *Film Architecture*, p. 96.

96 Florian Zimmermann (ed.), *Der Schrei nach dem Turmhaus* (Berlin: Bauhaus-Archiv, 1988) and Fritz Neumeier (ed.), *Ludwig Mies van der Rohe. Hochhaus am Bahnhof Friedrichstrasse* (Berlin: Ernst Wasmuth, 1993).

97 For a fuller discussion of these historical intertexts, see my 'Pleasure Gardens and Housing Problems: *Metropolis* and *Kuhle Wampe* in Context' and 'City of Light, Gardens of Delight: Fritz Lang's *Metropolis* and German Urbanism between Modernism and Modernisation', unpublished lectures, 1998 and 1999.

98 For a suggestive analogy between Lang's underground masses and various spontaneously combustible outsiders of the contemporary urban scene, such as Watts rioters, 'toons and penguins, see Peter Wollen, 'Metropolis and Batman Returns', *Sight and Sound*, July 1993, pp. 25–6.

99 'At Schwanecke's [a famous Berlin hangout] … what did they say about *Metropolis*? … that it is an artificial, coldly-calculated concoction, with glorious photography and hypocritical morals, with incredible technique and sentimental, pompous kitsch, with old and new tricks, terrible acting, atrocious dialogues, hollow symbolism, empty chatter, full of skewed realism and equally skewed romanticism, deeply dishonest in its subject, and entirely derived from well-known literary sources.' Fred Hildenbrandt, 'Metropolis', *Berliner Tageblatt* vol. 56 no. 17, 11 January 1927, evening edition.

100 Peter Sloterdijk, *Kritik der zynischen Vernunft* vol. 2 (Frankfurt: Suhrkamp, 1983), p. 708.

101 Almost every first-night review praises Fritz Rasp as 'Slim', commenting on his uncanny ubiquity and all-seeingness, one even calling him 'a perfect surveillance-machine' (*Licht-Bild-Bühne*, 11 January 1927).

102 In Eisenstein's *October* (1928) a similar scene is given a quite different meaning, or rather Lang, familiar with images of the storming of the Winter Palace, may have given his own iconic-ironic comment.

CREDITS

. . . .

Metropolis

Germany
1926
German Censorship
13 November 1926
(13,743 feet)
5 August 1927
(10,633 feet)
German Release
10 January 1927
Distributor
Parufamet

Production Company
Universum Film AG
(UFA) Berlin
Producer
Erich Pommer
Director
Fritz Lang
Screenplay
Fritz Lang,
Thea von Harbou
Based on an idea by
Thea von Harbou

Photography
Karl Freund,
Günther Rittau
**Schüfftan Process
Photography**
Helmar Lenski
Model Photography
Konstantin Irmen-Tschet
Stills
Horst von Harbou
Art Directors
Otto Hunte, Erich Kettelhut,
Karl Vollbrecht
Sculptures
Walter Schulze-Mittendorf
Costumes
Aenne Willkomm
**Original Accompanying
Score**
Gottfried Huppertz

Cast
Brigitte Helm
Maria / Robot Maria
Alfred Abel
Jon Fredersen
Gustav Fröhlich
Freder Fredersen
Rudolf Klein-Rogge
Rotwang
Fritz Rasp
Slim
Theodor Loos
Josaphat
Erwin Biswanger
No 11811
Heinrich George
Groth, machine foreman
Olaf Storm
Jan
Hanns Leo Reich
Marinus
Heinrich Gotho
master of ceremonies
Margarete Lanner
woman in car /
woman in Eternal Gardens

Max Dietze
Georg John
Walter Kühle
Arthur Reinhard
Erwin Vater
Grete Berger
Olly Böheim
Ellen Frey
Lisa Gray
Rose Liechtenstein
Helene Weigel
workers
Beatrice Garga
Anny Hintze
Helen von Münchhofen
Hilde Woitscheff
women in Eternal Garden
Fritz Alberti
creative man

Black and White
4189 metres 13,743 feet

Credits compiled by
Markku Salmi, BFI
Filmographic Unit

The print of *Metropolis* in
the National Film and
Television Archive is a high
quality positive produced
from material acquired over
the years from several
German film archives

BIBLIOGRAPHY

· ·

Albrecht, Donald, *Designing Dreams* (New York: Harper & Row, 1986), pp. 153–7.

Althen, Michael, 'Kunst im Bau', *Süddeutsche Zeitung*, 26 October 1988.

Antonietti, Paolo and Romana Schneider, 'Metropolis in Vitro', *Domus* no. 717, June 1990, pp. 74–80.

Arnheim, Rudolf, 'Metropolis', *Das Stachelschwein*, 1 February 1927, pp. 52–3.

Arns, Alfons and Hans Peter Reichmann (eds), *Otto Hunte: Architekt für den Film* (Frankfurt: Deutsches Filmmuseum, 1996).

Aubert, Michelle, 'Entretien sur Metropolis', *Positif* no. 421, March 1996, p. 89.

Beaton, Welford, 'Metropolis', *The Film Spectator*, 3 September 1927 [reprinted in Stanley `Kaufmann (ed.), *American Film Criticism from the Beginnings to Citizen Kane* (New York: Liveright, 1972), p. 189].

Beauplan, Robert de, 'La réalisation du film Metropolis', *La Petite Illustration* vol. 372, 3 March 1928 [Special number for the Paris premiere], p. 1.

Bellour, Raymond, 'On Fritz Lang', in S. Jenkins (ed.), *Fritz Lang, the Image and the Look* (London: British Film Institute, 1981), pp. 26–37.

Bertellini, Giorgio, 'Restauration, Genealogy, Palimpsests On Some Historiographical Questions', *Film History* vol. 7 no. 3, Autumn 1994, pp. 277–90.

Berthomé, Jean Pierre, 'Metropolis revisitée', *Positif* vol. 365–6, July–August 1991, pp. 94–8.

Beylie, Claude, 'Dédales de Metropolis', *Cinématographe*, July 1984, pp. 23–4.

Burch, Noel, 'Fritz Lang: German Period', in Richard Roud (ed.), *Cinema: A Critical Dictionary* vol. 2 (London: Secker & Warburg, 1980), pp. 583–99.

Bock, H. M. and M. Töteberg (eds), *Das Ufa Buch* (Frankfurt: Zweitausendeins, 1992).

Bogdanovich, Peter, *Fritz Lang in America* (London: Studio Vista, 1967).

Brennicke, Ilona and Joe Hembus, *Klassiker des deutschen Stummfilms* (Munich: Goldmann, 1983), pp. 134–42.

Buñuel, Luis, 'Metropolis', *La Gazeta Literaria*, 1 May 1927 [in English: Francisco Aranda, *Luis Buñuel: A Critical Biography* (New York: Da Capo Press, 1976)].

Cieutat, Brigitte, 'Le symbolisme des figures géometriques dans Metropolis', *Positif* 365–366, July–August 1991, pp. 133–6.

Codelli, Lorenzo, 'Entretien avec Enno Patalas', *Positif* vol. 285, November 1984, pp. 12–20.

Combs, Richard, 'Metropolis', *Monthly Film Bulletin* vol. 43 no. 507, April 1976, p. 91 and vol. 43 no. 508, May 1976, p. 112.

Dadoun, Roger, '*Metropolis*, Mère-Cité, Mittler, Hitler' *Revue Française de Psychanalyse*, January 1974 [in English: *Camera Obscura* vol. 15, 1986, pp. 137–64].

Domarchi, Jean and Jacques Rivette, 'Entretien avec Fritz Lang', *Cahiers du cinéma* vol. 99, September 1959.

Drummond, Ann, *Fritz Lang's Metropolis*, unpublished M.Phil. dissertation, University of Edinburgh, 1982.

Eggebrecht, Axel, 'Metropolis', *Die Weltbühne* vol. 3, 18 January 1927, p. 115.

Eggebrecht, Axel, 'Technik, Arbeit und Wissenschaft der Zukunft: Möglichkeiten eines Zukunftfilms', *Kulturwille* vol. 4 no. 6, 1927, pp. 123–5.

Eibel, Alfred (ed.), *Fritz Lang* (Paris: Le Terrain Vague, 1964).

Eisenschitz, Bernard, 'Metropolis, UFA et le cinéma allemand', in *Metropolis: Images d'un tournage* (Paris: Cinématèque française, 1985), pp. 139–42.

Eisner, Lotte, *Fritz Lang* (London: Secker & Warburg, 1976).

Elsaesser, Thomas, 'Innocence Restored', *Monthly Film Bulletin*, December 1984, pp. 363–6.

Elsaesser, Thomas, 'Endlosschleife Metropolis', in Irmbert Schenk (ed.), *Dschungel Großstadt. Kino und Modernisierung* (Marburg: Schüren, 1999), pp. 29–56.

Etten, Manfred, '"Aber ich interessierte mich für Maschinen…" 65 Jahre Metropolis: Rückblick auf eine Stadt der Zukunft', *Film-Dienst* vol. 45 no. 1, 7 January 1992, pp. 38–40.

Exner, Julian, 'Klassenkampf mit Musik', *Frankfurter Rundschau*, 5 April 1989.

Le film français, 'Metro, disco, Giorgio', 1997, 6 July 1984.

Freund, Karl, 'Meine Arbeit an *Metropolis*', *Berliner Zeitung*, 7 January 1927.

Gehler, Fred and Ullrich Kasten (eds), *Fritz Lang: die Stimme von Metropolis* (Berlin: Henschel, 1990).

Geser, Guntram, *Fritz Lang, Metropolis und Die Frau im Mond* (Meitingen: Corian, 1996).

Goettler, Fritz (ed.), *Fritz Lang Metropolis* (Munich: Stadtmuseum, 1988).

Grafe, Frieda, 'Für Fritz Lang. Ein Platz, kein Denkmal', in Frieda Grafe *et al.*, *Fritz Lang* (Munich: Hanser, 1976), pp. 7–82.

Grafe, Frieda, 'La Metropolis', in Bernard Eisenschitz and Paolo Bertetto (eds), *Fritz Lang. La Mise-en-Scène* (Turin: Lindau, 1993), pp. 117–20.

Guibert, Hervé, 'Saturday Night Metropolis', *Le Monde*, 8 August 1984.

Haas, Willy, 'Zwei große Filmpremieren: Metropolis, Hotel Stadt Lemberg', *Die Literarische Welt* 21 January 1927, p. 7.

von Harbou, Thea, *Metropolis* (Berlin: Scherl, 1926) [trans. London: Reader's Library, 1927].

von Harbou, Thea, 'Eine Szene wird geprobt', *Uhu* vol. 11, August 1926.

Hartmann, Siegfried, 'Metropolis-Technik', *Deutsche Allgemeine Zeitung*, 20 January 1927.

Heuss, Theodor, 'Metropolis', *Die Hilfe* vol. 33 no. 4, 15 December 1927, p. 108.

Hildenbrandt, Fred, 'Metropolis', *Berliner Tageblatt* vol. 56 no. 17, 11 January 1927, evening edition.

Hunte, Otto, 'Der Baumeister von Metropolis', *Illustrierter Film Kurier* 1927.

Huyssen, Andreas, 'The Vamp and the Machine: Technology and Sexuality in Fritz Lang's *Metropolis*', *New German Critique* vol. 24 no. 25, Fall/Winter 1981/2, pp. 221–37.

Ickes, Paul, 'Metropolis', *Die Filmwoche* vol. 3, 19 January 1927, p. 60.

Jacobs, Monty, 'Metropolis', *Vossische Zeitung*, 12 January 1927.

Jacques, Norbert, 'Metropolis', *Hannoverscher Anzeiger*, 21 January 1927.

Jenkins, Stephen, 'Lang: Fear and Desire', in S. Jenkins (ed.), *Fritz Lang, The Image and*

the Look (London: British Film Institute, 1981), pp. 82–7.

Jensen, Paul M., 'Metropolis – the Film and the Book', *Metropolis: A Film by Fritz Lang* (London: Lorrimer, 1973), pp. 5–14.

Jensen, Paul M., 'Metropolis', *Film Heritage* vol. 3 no. 2, Winter 1967–8.

Jhering, Herbert, 'Metropolis', *Berliner Börsen Courier*, 11 January 1927.

Kaes, Anton, 'Cinema and Modernity: On Fritz Lang's *Metropolis*', in R. Grimm and J. Hermand (eds), *High and Low. German Attempts at Mediation* (Madison: University of Wisconsin Press, 1994), pp. 19–33.

Kalbus, Oskar, *Vom Werden Deutscher Filmkunst*, vol. 1 (Altona: Cigaretten-Bilderdienst, 1935), pp. 96–102.

Kaplan, E. Ann, *Fritz Lang: A Guide to References and Resources* (Boston: G. K. Hall, 1981), pp. 145–54.

Keiner, Reinhold, *Thea von Harbou und der Deutsche Filme bis 1933* (Hildesheim: Georg Olms, 1984), pp. 91–100.

Kessler, Frank, *Metropolis de Fritz Lang: esthétique où esthétiques?*, doctoral thesis, Université de Paris III, 1988.

Kettelhut, Erich, 'Es wird anders gebaut', *Filmtechnik* vol. 16, 3 August 1929, p. 339.

Kettelhut, Erich, *Erinnerungen*, unpublished memoirs, Berlin: Stiftung Deutsche Kinemathek, 1960.

Knatz, Karlernst, 'Der Weltfilm der Ufa', *Tägliche Rundschau* vol. 47 no. 16, 11 January 1927.

Koerber, Martin, 'Notizen zur Überlieferung des Films *Metropolis*', in W. Jacobsen and W. Sudendorf (eds), *Metropolis. Aus dem Laboratorium der filmischen Moderne* (Stuttgart: Edition Menges, 2000).

Kracauer, Siegfried, *From Caligari to Hitler* (Princeton: Princeton University Press, 1947).

Kreimeier, Klaus, *Die Ufa Story* (Munich: Hanser, 1992).

Kriegk, Otto, *Der deutsche Film im Spiegel der Ufa. 25 Jahre Kampf und Vollendung* (Berlin: Ufa-Buchverlag, 1943), pp. 88–9.

Laberge, Yves, 'Le retour de Metropolis', *Etudes littéraires* vol. 18 no. 1, printemps/été 1985) pp. 135–54.

Lorant, Stephan (ed.), *Ufa Magazin Sondernummer Metropolis*, January 1927.

Lydor, Waldemar, 'Berliner Zickzack', *Dortmunder Generalanzeiger*, 17 January 1927.

Maibohm, Ludwig, 'Amerika-Trip mit Folgen', in *Fritz Lang, Seine Filme – Sein Leben* (Munich: Heyne, 1981), pp. 78–105.

McGilligan, Patrick, *Fritz Lang. The Nature of the Beast* (New York: St. Martin's Press, 1997).

Mellencamp, Patricia, 'Oedipus and the Robot in *Metropolis*', *Enclitic* vol. 5 no. 1, Spring 1981, pp. 20–42.

Minichiello, Peter, 'Introduction' to Thea von Harbou, *Metropolis* (Boston: G. K. Hall, 1975), pp. 5–15.

Moebius, Hanno and Guntram Vogt, *Drehort Stadt. Das Thema 'Großstadt' im deutschen Film* (Marburg: Hitzeroth, 1990).

Neumann, Dietrich, 'The Urbanist Vision of Fritz Lang's Metropolis', in Thomas Kniesche and Stephan Brockmann (eds), *Dancing on the Volcano* (New York: Columbia University Press, 1994), pp. 133–62.

Neumann, Dietrich (ed.), *Film Architecture. From Metropolis to Blade Runner* (Munich: Prestel, 1996), pp. 33–46 and 94–103.

E. S. P., 'Metropolis', *Licht-Bild-Bühne*, 11 January 1927.

Patalas, Enno, 'Metropolis, Scene 103', *Camera Obscura* vol. 15, 1986, pp. 165–73.

Patalas, Enno, 'Metropolis – Die Zukunftsstadt – ein Trümmerfilm', in Irmbert Schenk (ed.), *Dschungel Großstadt. Kino und Modernisierung* (Marburg: Schüren, 1999), pp. 15–28.

Petro, Patrice, *Writings in Film History: The German Cinema and Metropolis*, unpublished M.A. thesis, University of California, Santa Barbara, 1982.

Phillipe, Claude-Jean, 'Analyse d'un grand film: Metropolis', *Télérama*, 24 October 1965, pp. 79–80.

Pinel, Vincent, 'Pour une déontologie de la restauration des films', *Positif* vol. 421, March 1996, pp. 90–3.

Pinthus, Kurt, 'Lemberg und Metropolis', *Das Tage-Buch*, 15 January 1927, pp. 97–103.

Pynchon, Thomas, *Gravity's Rainbow* (New York: Bantam Books, 1972).

Quaresima, Leonardo, 'Ninon, la hermana de Maria. Metropolis y sus variantes', *Archivos de la Filmoteca de Valencia* vol. 17, June 1994, pp. 5–37.

Rabenalt, Peter, 'Nicht nur Metropolis … Filmmusik live als neues "altes" Filmerlebnis?', *Film und Fernsehen* vol. xx no. 3, June 1992, pp. 38–40.

Rittau, Günther, 'Die Trickaufnahmen im Metropolis Film', *Deutsche Filmwoche*, 28 January 1927, p. 10.

Roth, Lane, '*Metropolis* The Light Fantastic', *Literature/Film Quarterly* vol. 6 no. 4, 1978, pp. 342–6.

Roy, Jean, 'Le lifting de Fritz', *L'Humanité*, 8 August 1984.

Salt, Barry, 'From Caligari to Who?', *Sight and Sound*, Spring 1979, pp. 119–23.

Schacht, Roland [Balthasar], 'Der Metropolis Film', *Das Blaue Heft* vol. 9 no. 3, 1 February 1927, pp. 73–6.

Schacht, Roland, 'Der Metropolisfilm der Ufa', *Der Kunstwart* vol. 40 no. 5, 1927, pp. 341–2.

Schenk, Irmbert, 'Moderne, Avantgarde, Postmoderne', *Impulse aus der Forschung* vol. 12, October 1991, pp. 45–9.

Schneider, Roland, 'Au-delá de l'expressionisme: la vision architecturale de Fritz Lang' *CinémAction* vol. 75, April 1995, pp. 25–33.

Schönemann, Heide, *Fritz Lang: Filmbilder Vorbilder* (Berlin: Hentrich, 1992).

Siemsen, Hans, 'Eine Filmkritik wie sie sein soll,' *Die Weltbühne* vol. 23 no. 4,14 June 1927, pp. 947–50.

Simmon, Scott, 'Gravity's Rainbow as Film', *Literature/Film Quarterly* vol. 6 no. 4, 1978, pp. 347–51.

Sturm, Georges, 'Auf der Suche nach der verlorenen Szene', *Bulletin Cicim* vol. 5–6, 1983, pp. 88–95.

Sturm, Georges, 'Für Hel ein Denkmal', *Bulletin Cicim* vol. 9, 1984.

Töteberg, Michael, *Fritz Lang* (Reinbek: Rowohlt, 1985).

Treuner, Hermann, 'Der Künstliche Mensch', *Deutsche Filmwoche*, 21 January 1927, p. 1.

Tulloch, John, ` Genetic Structuralism and the Cinema: A Look at Fritz Lang's Metropolis', *Australian Journal of Screen Theory* vol. 1, 1976, pp. 3–50.

Tyler, Parker, 'Metropolis', in *Classics of the Foreign Film* (New York: Bonanza, 1962), pp. 38–40.

UFA GmbH, *Presse-und Propagandaheft Metropolis*, January 1927.

Vitoux, Frederic, 'Un rocker nommé Fritz Lang', *Le Nouvel Observateur*, August 1984.

Weihsmann, Helmut, *Gebaute Illusionen: Architektur im Film* (Vienna: Promedia, 1988), pp. 171–7.

Wells, H. G., 'Mr Wells Reviews a Current Film', *New York Times*, 17 April 1927, pp. 4, 22.

Wiener, Thomas, 'Oh, No, Giogio', *American Film*, May 1984, p. 8.

Williams, Alan, 'Structures of Narrativity in Fritz Lang's Metropolis', *Film Quarterly* vol. 27 no. 4, Summer 1974, pp. 17–23.

Wollen, Peter, 'Cinema/Americanism/The Robot', *New Formations* vol. 8, 1989, pp. 7–34.

Ziege, Felix, 'Metropolis und wir', *Kulturwille* vol. 4 no. 6,1927, p. 125.

ALSO PUBLISHED

If you would like further information about future BFI Film Classics or about other books from BFI Publishing, please sign up to our mailing list at www.palgrave.com/bfi.

You can also write to:
**BFI/Palgrave Macmillan Ltd
Houndmills
Basingstoke
RG21 6XS UK**